# LES GUÉRILLÈRES

MONIQUE WITTIG

# *Les Guérillères*

Translated from the French by

David Le Vay

BEACON PRESS · BOSTON

Copyright ©1969 by Les Editions de Minuit
English translation copyright ©1971 by Peter Owen
Published by The Viking Press, Inc., in 1971
First published as a Beacon paperback in 1985

Beacon Press books are published under the auspices
of the Unitarian Universalist Association of
Congregations in North America,
25 Beacon Street, Boston, Massachusetts 02108
Published simultaneously in Canada by
Fitzhenry and Whiteside Limited, Toronto

Printed in the United States of America

(paperback) 9


Library of Congress Cataloging in Publication Data

Wittig, Monique.
    Les guérillères.

        Reprint.    Originally published: London : P. Owen, 1971.
        Title.
[PQ2683.I8G813    1985]    843'.914        85-6150
ISBN 0-8070-6301-0 (pbk.)

GOLDEN SPACES LACUNAE
THE GREEN DESERTS ARE SEEN
THEY DREAM AND SPEAK OF THEM
THE IMMOBILE BIRDS OF JET
THE WEAPONS PILED IN THE SUN
THE SOUND OF THE SINGING VOICES
THE DEAD WOMEN THE DEAD WOMEN

CONSPIRACIES REVOLUTIONS
FERVOUR FOR THE STRUGGLE
INTENSE HEAT DEATH AND HAPPINESS
IN THE BREASTED TORSOS
THE PHOENIXES THE PHOENIXES
FREE CELIBATE GOLDEN
THEIR OUTSPREAD WINGS ARE HEARD

THE BIRDS THE SWIMMING SIRENS
THE TRANSLUCENT SPANS THE WINGS
THE GREEN SUNS THE GREEN SUNS
THE VIOLET FLAT GRASSLANDS
THE CRIES THE LAUGHS THE MOVE-
    MENTS
THE WOMEN AFFIRM IN TRIUMPH THAT
ALL ACTION IS OVERTHROW

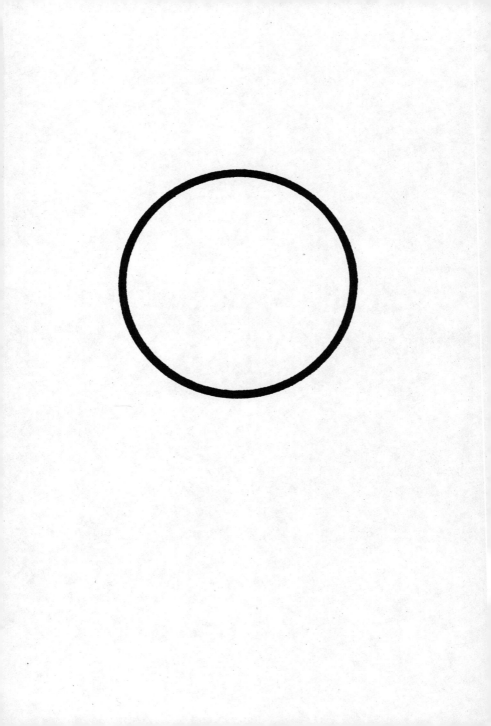

When it rains the women stay in the summer-house. They hear the water beating on the tiles and streaming down the slopes of the roof. Fringes of rain surround the summer-house, the water that runs down at its angles flows more strongly, it is as if springs hollow out the pebbles at the places where it reaches the ground. At last someone says it is like the sound of micturition, that she cannot wait any longer, and squats down. Then some of them form a circle around her to watch the labia expel the urine.

The women frighten each other by hiding behind the trees. One or other of them asks for grace. Then they chase each other in the darkness, ill-wishing the one who is caught. Or else they search gropingly, scenting the one whose perfume is to be honoured. Amomum aniseed betel cinnamon cubeb mint liquorice musk ginger clove nutmeg pepper saffron sage vanilla receive homage in turn. Then the wearers of these perfumes are chased in the dark as in blindman's-buff. Cries laughter sounds of falling are heard.

In dull weather the women may shed hot tears, saying that in the sunshine the roofs of the houses and the walls are of quite another colour. Mist spreads over the water over the fields about the houses. It penetrates through closed windows. Someone arrives to visit the house. She cannot see it. The huge paintings in vivid colours disappear behind orange vapours. Then she slumps to the ground demanding to be entertained. They tell her in great detail the story of the woman who, speaking of her vulva, used to say that thanks to that compass she could navigate from sunrise to sunset.

Some of the women swim letting themselves drift toward the last splashes of sunlight on the sea. At the most luminous spot when, dazzled, they try to move away, they say that they are assailed by an unbearable stench. Later they are seized with vomiting. Then they begin to moan as they strain their arms, swimming as fast as they can. At a certain point they collide with the floating decaying carcase of an ass, at times the swell of the sea reveals sticky shapeless gleaming lumps of indescribable colour. They say that they shouted with all their might, shedding many tears, complaining that no sea-breeze got up to drive away the smell, supporting under the arms and groins one of them who has fainted, while the vomit accumulates around them on the surface of the water.

If anyone walks on the hillside she can hardly remain upright. Through the hedges white colchicum and violets or pink-capped mushrooms can be seen. The grass is not tall. Heifers stand in it, in great number. The houses have been shuttered since the autumn rains began. There are no little girls playing in the gardens. There are no flowers in the flower-beds. A few toys lie about, a painted wooden hoop a red and blue olisbos a white balloon a lead rifle.

The women visit the market to obtain provisions. They pass by the stalls of fruit vegetables bottles of pink blue red green glass. There are piles of orange oranges ochre pineapples mandarines walnuts green and pink mangos blue nectarines green and pink peaches orange-yellow apricots. There are melons water-melons paw-paws avocados green almonds medlars. There are cucumbers aubergines cabbages asparagus white cassava red pimentos gourds. Wasps coming and going settle on the bare arms of the young women selling them.

The huntresses have dark maroon hats, and dogs. Hearing the rifle-shots, Dominique Aron says that the bird is still flying, the hare still running, the boar the deer the fox the wart-hog still afoot. It is possible to keep a watch on the surroundings. If some troop advances up the road raising a cloud of dust the women watch its approach shouting to those within for the windows to be closed and the rifles kept behind the windows. Anne Damien plays, Sister Anne do you see anything coming, I see only the grass growing green and the dusty road.

At evening a horse harnessed to a cart goes by. The cart carries a heap of cut beetroots or potatoes or grass for fodder. Long before and long after it passes the sound of the hooves striking the tarred road can be heard. The horse on its way is not being driven by anyone.

THAT WHICH IDENTIFIES THEM LIKE
THE EYE OF THE CYCLOPS,
THEIR SINGLE FORENAME,
OSEA BALKIS SARA NICEA
IOLA CORA SABINA DANIELA
GALSWINTHA EDNA JOSEPHA

Somewhere there is a siren. Her green body is covered with scales. Her face is bare. The undersides of her arms are a rosy colour. Sometimes she begins to sing. The women say that of her song nothing is to be heard but a continuous O. That is why this song evokes for them, like everything that recalls the O, the zero or the circle, the vulval ring.

By the lakeside there is an echo. As they stand there with an open book the chosen passages are re-uttered from the other side by a voice that becomes distant and repeats itself. Lucie Maure cries to the double echo the phrase of Phénarète, I say that that which is is. I say that that which is not also is. When she repeats the phrase several times the double, then triple, voice endlessly superimposes that which is and that which is not. The shadows brooding over the lake shift and begin to shiver because of the vibrations of the voice.

The women are seen to have in their hands small books which they say are feminaries. These are either multiple copies of the same original or else there are several kinds. In one of them someone has written an inscription which they whisper in each other's ears and which provokes them to full-throated laughter. When it is leafed through the feminary presents numerous blank pages in which they write from time to time. Essentially, it consists of pages with words printed in a varying number of capital letters. There may be only one or the pages may be full of them. Usually they are isolated at the centre of the page, well spaced black on a white background or else white on a black background.

After the sun has risen they anoint their bodies with oil of sandalwood curcuma gardenia. They steady one foot on a tree-trunk. Their hands rub each leg in turn, the skin glistening. Some of them are lying down. Others massage them with their fingertips. The bare bodies gleam in the strong morning light. One of their flanks is iridescent with a golden lustre. The rising sun does likewise when it sends its rays slanting across the erect rounded tree-trunks. The arcs of the circles so touched reflect a little of the light, their outlines are blurred.

There are peat-bogs above the hills. The mud they are made of has the colour of henna. They seethe, there are surface explosions, bubbles. A stick stirred around within them is caught by viscous soft bodies. It is not possible to fish these out. As soon as any pressure is exerted on them they slip away, they escape. The women say that at times the bursting of the bubbles is accompanied by groans murmurs. The sun dries up the bogs. The vapour that ascends then has a nauseating odour.

The gipsy women have a mummified corpse which they bring out when it is not raining, because of the smell of the body which is not quite dry. They expose it to the sun in its box. The dead woman is clothed in a long tunic of green velvet, covered with white embroidery and gilded ornaments. They have hung little bells on her neck, on her sleeves. They have put medallions in her hair. When they take hold of the box to bring it out the dead woman begins to tinkle everywhere. Every now and then someone goes out on to the three steps that lead up to the caravan to look at the clouds. When the sky is obscured two of them set about shutting the lid of the box and carrying it inside.

FLORA ZITA SAVA CORNELIA
DRAUPADI JULIENNE ETMEL
CHLOË DESDEMONA RAPHAELA
IRIS VERA ARSINOË LISA
BRENDA ORPHISE HERODIAS
BERENICE SIGRID ANDOVERA

The little girls search in the bushes and trees for the nests of goldfinches chaffinches linnets. They find some green canaries which they cover with kisses, which they hug to their breasts. They run singing, they bound over the rocks. A hundred thousand of them return to their houses to cherish their birds. In their haste they clasped them too tightly to themselves. They ran. They bent down to pick up pebbles which they cast far away over the hedges. They took no heed of their chirping. They climbed straight up to their rooms. They removed the birds from their garments, they found them lifeless, heads drooping. Then they all tried to revive them by pressing them to their mouths, letting their warm breath fall on them, lifting the limp heads, touching their beaks with a finger. They remained inert. Then a hundred thousand little girls bewailed the death of their green canaries in the hundred thousand rooms of the hundred thousand houses.

Whatever the time appointed to begin the work, they must hurry to get finished before sunset. The bottoms of the ladders are visible placed on the ground, the tops are hidden in the jumble of fruit and foliage. The baskets at the foot of the trees are filled at times to overflowing. There are *belles de Choisy* English cherries morellos marascas Montmorency cherries *bigaudelles* white-hearts. They are black white red translucent. Wasps hornets are busy around the baskets. Their buzzing can be heard in whatever part of the meadow one happens to be. The women climb into the trees, they descend arms laden with fruit. Some have baskets hooked to their belt. Some stand still at different heights on the rungs. Others move about among the branches. One sees them jump to the ground and get rid of their burden. The slanting rays of the sun glance over the leaves making them glitter. The sky is orange-coloured.

The women say that they expose their genitals so that the sun may be reflected therein as in a mirror. They say that they retain its brilliance. They say that the pubic hair is like a spider's web that captures the rays. They are seen running with great strides. They are all illuminated at their centre, starting from the pubes the hooded clitorides the folded double labia. The glare they shed when they stand still and turn to face one makes the eye turn elsewhere unable to stand the sight.

When the moon is full the drum is sounded on the main square. Trestle tables are erected. Glasses of every colour are put out and bottles containing differently coloured liquids. Some of these liquids are green red blue, they evaporate if they are not used as soon as the cork that seals them has been drawn. Everyone may drink until she falls dead-drunk or until she has lost her self-control. The odour of the drugs which have been allowed to escape from the bottles stagnates on the square, sickeningly sweet. Everyone drinks in silence standing or lying down on carpets unrolled in the street. Then they have the little girls brought out. They are seen standing half asleep bewildered hesitant. They are invited to try their strength on the whimpering outstretched bodies. The children go from one to the other trying to wake them up, using stones buckets of water, shouting with all their might, squatting down to be at the level of the ears of the sleeping women.

Marthe Vivonne and Valerie Céru make a report. They say that the river is rising up between its banks. The fields of flowers by its banks are swept away by the waters. Avulsed corollas, upside down, eddy capsized in the current. All along the river there is an odour of putrescence. A noise like that of a broken flood-gate is heard. Overturned boats drift by. Whole trees are carried away, their fruit-laden branches trailing in the water. Marthe Vivonne and Valerie Céru say they have not seen any corpses of animals. They say that for a long while on the way back they heard the rushing of the river, the shock of the current against its bed.

AIMEE POMA BARBA
BENEDICTA SUSANNA
CASSANDRA OSMONDA
GENE HERMINIA KIKA
AURELIA EVANGELINE
SIMONA MAXIMILIANA

The excursions with the glenuri on their leashes are not
without difficulty. Their long filiform bodies are supported on thousands of feet. They constantly endeavour
to move away to some place other than where they are.
Their innumerable eyes are grouped round an enormous
orifice that serves them as a mouth as well as taking the
place of a head. It is filled by a soft extensile membrane
that can become taut or relaxed, each of its movements
producing a different sound. The harmony of the glenuri
may be compared to fifes drums the croaking of toads
the miaowing of rutting cats the sharp sound of a flute.
The excursions with the glenuri are constantly being
interrupted. This is because they systematically insinuate
themselves into any interstice that affords passage to
their bodies, for example the gates of public gardens, the
grills of drains. They enter these backwards, they are
stopped at a given moment by the size of their heads,
they find themselves trapped, they begin to utter fright-
ful shrieks. Then they have to be freed.

The women say that in the feminary the glans of the
clitoris and the body of the clitoris are described as

hooded. It is stated that the prepuce at the base of the glans can travel the length of the organ exciting a keen sensation of pleasure. They say that the clitoris is an erectile organ. It is stated that it bifurcates to right and left, that it is angled, extending as two erectile bodies applied to the pubic bones. These two bodies are not visible. The whole constitutes an intensely erogenous zone that excites the entire genital, making it an organ impatient for pleasure. They compare it to mercury also called quicksilver because of its readiness to expand, to spread, to change shape.

Daniela Nervi, while digging foundations, has unearthed a painting representing a young girl. She is all flat and white lying on one side. She has no clothes. Her breasts are barely visible on her torso. One of her legs, crossed over the other, raises her thigh, so concealing the pubis and vulva. Her long hair hides part of her shoulders. She is smiling. Her eyes are closed. She half leans on one elbow. The other arm is crooked over her head, the hand holding a bunch of black grapes to her mouth. The women laugh at this. They say that Daniela Nervi has not yet dug up the knife without a blade that lacks a handle.

Martha Ephore has made all the calculations. The engineers were mistaken. Or else the water arriving from the mountain slopes is insufficient to feed the lake beyond the barrage, even in time of spate. Or else they have been at fault over the position of the construction which they have sited too far upstream in relation to the junction of the water-courses. Every morning the engineers arrive at the dam which they patrol in all directions, marking the still fresh cement with the imprint of their feet, so that after they leave a team of masons have to busy themselves getting rid of them. Some of the women run with umbrellas held high, giving orders. Others walk about calmly. By the shore of the lake or what ought to be the lake young girls in bermudas stroll about holding each other by the hand.

The women say that the goddess Eristikos has a pin head and yellow eyes. They say that the goddess Eristikos adores perfumes. In her honour they wear next the skin garments made of fragrant herbs. They set them on fire at nightfall by putting a light to each sprig. They are grouped in circles, their garments are incandescent in the darkness. They stand motionless, arms extended on either side of their bodies. The burning herbs crackle' and give off an odour. Smoke clouds disperse. When the heat reaches the skin they savagely tear off their tunics and cast them in a heap. That is why they must continually manufacture new ones.

24

CALYPSO JUDITH ANNE
ISEULT KRISTA ROBERTA
VLASTA CLEONICE RENEE
MARIA BEATRICE REINA
IDOMENEA GUILHERMINA
ARMIDE ZENOBIA LESSIA

There exists a machine to record divergences. It is placed on an agate plinth. This is a parallelepipedon of low stature, at the centre of a meadow studded with daisies in spring, marguerites in summer, white and blue saffron in the autumn. The calculations taking place within the machine are continuously registered as clicks clicking high-pitched sounds as of tinkling bells, noises like those of a cash-register. There are lights that go out and come on at irregular intervals of time. They are red orange blue. The apertures through which they shine are circular. Every divergence is ceaselessly recorded in the machine. They are scaled to the same unit whatever their nature. The position in the field of the machine for recording divergences resembles that of a certain fountain guarded by young girls bearing flaming swords. But the machine is not guarded. It is easy of access.

The women recall the story of the one who lived for a long time where the camels pass. Bareheaded beneath the sun, Clemence Maïeul incessantly invokes Amaterasu the sun goddess, cutting her abundant hair, abasing herself three times on the ground which she strikes with her hands, saying, I salute you, great Amaterasu, in the name of our mother, in the name of those who are to come. Our kingdom come. May this order be destroyed. May the good and the evil be cast down. They say that Clemence Maïeul often drew on the ground that O which is the sign of the goddess, symbol of the vulval ring.

The women say that any one of them might equally well invoke another sun goddess, such as Cihuacoatl, who is also a goddess of war. Thus on the occasion of the death of one of their number they might use the song of mourning which is a glorious song. Then they sing in unison, Strong and warlike daughter, my well-beloved daughter/valiant and tender little dove, my lady/you have striven and worked as a valiant daughter/you have overcome, you have acted like your mother the lady Cihuacoatl/you have fought with valour, you have used shield and sword/arise my daughter/go to that good place which is the house of your mother the sun/where all are filled with joy content and happiness.

The women leap on the paths that lead to the village, shaking their hair, their arms laden with dog-faced baboons, stamping the ground with their feet. Someone stops, tears out a handful of her long hair and lets the strands go one by one with the wind. Like the balloons that little girls release on holidays, rising into the sky, light unsubstantial filiform and twisting, they are blown upward by the wind. Or perhaps the women sing in unison a song that includes these words, Who till now sucked at my nipple/a monkey. Then they throw down all the baboons and begin to run, chasing them into the shade of the wood until they have disappeared in the trees.

They say, how to decide that an event is worthy of remembrance? Must Amaterasu herself advance on the forecourt of the temple, her face shining, blinding the eyes of those who, prostrate, put their foreheads to the ground and dare not lift their heads? Must Amaterasu raising her circular mirror on high blaze forth with all her fires? Must the rays from her slanting mirror set fire to the ground beneath the feet of the women who have come to pay homage to the sun goddess, the greatest of the goddesses? Must her anger be exemplary?

IDO BLANCHE VALENTINA
GILBERTA FAUSTA MONIMA
GE BAUCIS SOPHIE ALICE
OCTAVIA JOSIANA GAIA
DEODATA KAHA VILAINE
ANGE FREDERICA BETJE

The women say that references to Amaterasu or Cihua-coatl are no longer in order. They say they have no need of myths or symbols. They say that the time when they started from zero is in process of being erased from their memories. They say they can barely relate to it. When they repeat, This order must be destroyed, they say they do not know what order is meant.

What was the beginning? they say. They say that in the beginning they are huddled against each other. They are like black sheep. They open their mouths to bleat or to say something but no sound emerges. Their hair their curls are plastered against their foreheads. They move over the smooth shining surface. Their movements are translation, gliding. They are dazed by the reflections over which they pass. Their limbs gain no adhesion any-where. Vertically and horizontally, it is the same mirror neither hot nor cold, it is the same brilliance which no-where holds them fast. They advance, there is no front, there is no rear. They move on, there is no future, there is no past. They move flung one against the other. The movements they initiate with their lower limbs or with their upper limbs multiply the changes of position. If there had been an initial change of position it would be a fact that contradicted their unchanging functioning. It would be a fundamental variation that contradicted the unitary system, it would introduce disorder. They come and go ensheathed in something black and glitter-ing. The silence is absolute. If sometimes they try to stop to listen to something, the sound of a train, a ship's siren, the music of X X, their attempt to halt propels them from one side to the other, makes them sway, gives them a fresh departure. They are prisoners of the mirror.

The women say that the feminary amuses the little girls. For instance three kinds of labia minora are mentioned there. The dwarf labia are triangular. Side by side, they form two narrow folds. They are almost invisible because the labia majora cover them. The moderate-sized labia minora resemble the flower of a lily. They are half-moon shaped or triangular. They can be seen in their entirety taut supple seething. The large labia spread out resemble a butterfly's wings. They are tall triangular or rectangular, very prominent.

They say that as possessors of vulvas they are familiar with their characteristics. They are familiar with the mons pubis the clitoris the labia minora the body and bulbs of the vagina. They say that they take a proper pride in that which has for long been regarded as the emblem of fecundity and the reproductive force in nature.

They say that the clitoris has been compared to a cherry-stone, a bud, a young shoot, a shelled sesame, an almond, a sprig of myrtle, a dart, the barrel of a lock. They say that the labia majora have been compared to the two halves of a shellfish. They say that the concealed face of the labia minora has been compared to the purple of Sidon, to tropic coral. They say that the secretion has been compared to iodized salt water.

They say that they have found inscriptions on plaster walls where vulvas have been drawn as children draw suns with multiple divergent rays. They say that it has been written that vulvas are traps vices pincers. They say that the clitoris has been compared to the prow of a boat to its stem to the comb of a shellfish. They say that vulvas have been compared to apricots pomegranates figs roses pinks peonies marguerites. They say these comparisons may be recited like a litany.

OTTONE KAMALA POMARA
SIGISMUNDA MARCELINA
GALATEA ZAIRE EVELINA
CONSTANCE ANNUNCIATA
VICTORIA MARGUERITE
ROSE JULIA AGLAË LEDA

Anemone Flavien tells them the story of the woman selling pins who knocks at the young girl's door. When the young girl opens the window and leans out the white cat glides before her face, which makes her cry out. Her hair hangs down on the side towards which she leans. Then the merchant woman presents her with pins in her open hands. They have green red blue heads. When the woman catches her foot she drops all the pins between the separate paving-stones. The young girl complains loudly that her attire will be ruined. A little girl passing by sets about picking up the red green blue pins, when she gets up she puts them in the hands of the merchant woman. The pin-seller lifts her head to heaven, she begins to run opening her hands, laughing with all her might, scattering the green red blue pins everywhere, the little girl hops along behind her, while the young woman begins to utter piercing cries at her window.

Or else the women play a game. There is a whole row of toads with staring eyes. They are motionless. The first to feel a kick rolls over on its side in one piece like a mannequin stuffed with straw and without a sound. The others go jumping away. Their backs can be seen from time to time above the lucerne and the pink clover. They are like fat hens, heads lowered, pecking and looking at the ground. They do not progress evenly. Some of the faster ones are far ahead. One of them disappears in the hedge. It is soon followed by others, except for one solitary one that continues to roam in the fields.

Or else three cats are caught by the tail in a trap. They each go their own way miaowing. The heavy trap jerks forward slowly behind them. They scream, they lash out, scratching the ground with their claws. Their hair is on end. One of them stands still and begins to arch its back grinding its teeth and shrieking. The two other cats strive to shake him off by tugging at the trap. But they only succeed in making him turn a somersault in the iron collar. Then all three fight each other, they fling themselves against each other scratching and biting, they wound each other's eyes, their muzzles, they tear the hair from their necks, they can no longer stop fighting and the trap which gets between their legs only adds to their fury.

Fabienne Jouy tells a story about wolves. It begins thus: The glazed snow glistens. She says that it takes place at sunset. It continues like this: The sun is red, low in the sky, enormous. The stretched-out bodies do not stir. A feeble gleam of light comes from the weapons piled nearby. The first howls of the wolves are heard before sundown. They are far away scattered far apart. They are howling. They are nearby. Shadows come and go, flitting under the trees, leave the shelter of the woods, approach, retreat. The howling of the wolves never stops. The still bodies lying on the snow are joined by the hesitating moving mass of wolves. Ears erect, paws aquiver, they are above the faces, they sniff at the cheeks, the mouths, they come and go, they make a rush. The faces are torn to ribbons. The white face of the beautiful Marie Viarme hangs detached from the trunk, torn across at the throat. One sees the sudden streaming of blood on her cheeks. Clothes are torn, half-eaten bodies swim in a vile red-black lake, the snow is tinged by it. The wolves pant, they come and go, abandoning a body, seizing it anew, running to another, paws aquiver, tongues lolling. The wolves' eyes begin to shine in the half light. Fabienne Jouy has finished her story when she says, It is not known which way the wind was blowing. Comment is not advisable after someone has told a story. Despite this Cornélie Surger cannot refrain from saying, To hell with stories of wolves, now if it had had to do with rats, yes if only they had been rats.

The women break the walnuts to extract their oil. They take the fragments to the press where they are crushed. The kernels are arranged on the grindstone. The long wooden screw that turns the grindstone is iron-tipped. Trickles of oil overflow. At the same time they crush sesame poppy seeds. The petals of macerated flowers,

AUBIERGE CLARISSA PHÆDRA
EUDOXIA OLIVE IO MODESTA
PLAISANCE HYGEIA LOUISA
CORALIE ANEMONE TABITHA
THELMA INGRID PRASCOVIA
NATALIE POMPEIA ALIENOR

pinks herbs mallows are crushed by the grindstone. The white perfumed flowers of the myrtle also serve for the preparation of an oil which is the water of the angels. It is collected in a stone flask. Oily vapours move about in the overheated room. The walls are greasy, sweating. The women let down their hair, they soak it in the aromatic baths. Their hands and arms glisten, their breasts are bare.

The banks of the river are muddy. The black water seems deep. It is not possible to touch the bottom with a stick. Pale blue water-irises, red water-lilies cling to the roots of the trees that overhang the bank. The heads of the swimming women appear down below in the middle of the river, they are confused with their reflections in the water. A black barge moving up-river is always on the point of touching them. The swimmers touched, so it seems, sink. But their heads reappear, round, bobbing in the wash. The long strident whistle of a lock-keeper makes itself heard. There is smoke somewhere upstream. The sun is no longer visible. The water becomes darker and darker until it has lost its fluid appearance.

The women look at the old pictures, the photographs. One of them explains. For instance the series of the textile factory. There is a strike that day. The women workers form a picket line in the field where the buildings are sited. They move in a circle one behind the other singing stamping their feet on the ground clapping their hands. They have black blouses and woollen scarves. All the windows, all the doors of the factory are closed. One or other of them carries at arm's length a placard on which slogans are written, painted in red on the white paper. Under their feet in the field is a circle of beaten earth.

Or else someone comments on the series of photographs of demonstrations. The women demonstrators advance all holding a book in their upraised hands. The faces are remarkable for their beauty. Their compact mass bursts into the square, quickly but without violence, borne by the impetus intrinsic to its size. Great commotions take place at various points in the square when the demonstrators attempt to halt around groups of one or more speakers. But they are immediately pushed dragged along by the thousands of young women who follow them and who stop in their turn. Despite the disturbance of the general order created by individual movements there is no trampling underfoot, there are no shouts, there are no sudden violent rushes, the speakers are able to stay put. At a certain point the whole crowd begins to come to a halt. It takes some time for it to come to a complete standstill. Over to one side speeches have commenced, voices over the loud-speakers claim the attention of the demonstrators.

The cranes have laid bare the rootlets of a tree. With grabs they have unearthed the brittle filiform curled extremities. Shrivelled shrunken decaying leaves are attached to them. Systematically demarcating the zones from which the tree is nourished they have arrived at the centre of the tree, the trunk. They have freed the buried tree completely, branches leaves trunk roots. The eroded whitened trunk seems almost transparent. Branches and roots look alike. From the main branches and roots there come off twigs that form a complicated tangled network, sparsely cluttered in places by a few leaves, a few fruits.

The water party is heralded by a rattle of very hard wood, box or sandalwood, which, shaken, makes a discordant noise. The water is collected in vats of enormous capacity. Others are situated in cellars invaded by the tide. As a general rule there is always plenty of water.

40

It is used to soak the ground before undertaking any construction. It is thus that the outlines of secondary roads can be laid down, trenches dug, new terraces built, roundabouts constructed.

Laure Jamais begins her story with, *Plume, plume l'escargot, petit haricot*. It is about Iris Our. Laure Jamais says, is she or is she not dead? Her nerves relax. She moves more feebly. The severed carotid releases gushes of blood. There is some on her white garments. It has flowed over her breast, it has spread, there is some on her hands. Though bright, it seems thickened and coagulated. Clots have formed crusts on her clothes. Iris Our's arms dangle on either side. Her legs are outstretched. A fly comes and settles. Later it can be heard still buzzing. The window is open, on its other side there stir the branches of a pale green acacia. The sky is not to be seen. Iris Our's eyes are closed. There is a sort of smile on her lips, her teeth are bared. Later the smile broadens, it is the beginning of a laugh. However the severed carotid allows no sound to form at her lips, save for a gurgling attributable to the swallowing of blood.

The first women to swim up the river make the flying-fish jump. They have rounded saffron-coloured bodies. They are seen rising up out of the water, lifting themselves. They fall back noisily. Everywhere the fish begin to leave the water. At a certain point the swimming women find themselves in the shallows. Their hands and feet encounter fishy bodies, make them leap up. Between the pale blue sky and the ochre water there are the red bodies of fish moving away, leaping.

The women look at the old colour engraving. Someone says of it, these are women in royal blue uniform marching in platoon. There are fifteen of them. Their trousers have a black stripe at the side. The uniforms have gilt buttons. They advance to the sound of the music of a fife. Above their heads the trees are tossed by the wind. White acacia blossom and lime blossom fall on their heads. One of the women begins to laugh. On the square the noise of the fountain is so great that it drowns the music. But, whether because the musicians have re-doubled their efforts or because they are a match for the fountain, at a certain point the sound of the water is only faintly heard. The windows of the houses are open. No heads appear in them. The women traverse the length of the main street and halt under the arcades. Their marching order is broken. They enter chattering and the people in the café, turning their heads towards them, regard them. In the midst of the royal blue uniforms there is a woman clothed entirely in red, also in uniform.

DEMONA EPONINA GABRIELA
FULVIA ALEXANDRA JUSTINE
PHILOMELA CELINE HELENA
PHILIPPINA ZOË HORTENSE
SOR DOMINIQUE ARABELLA
MARJOLAINE LOIS ARMANDA

As regards the feminaries the women say for instance that they have forgotten the meaning of one of their ritual jokes. It has to do with the phrase, The bird of Venus takes flight towards evening. It is written that the lips of the vulva have been compared to the wings of a bird, hence the name of bird of Venus that has been given them. The vulva has been compared to all·kinds of birds, for instance to doves, starlings, bengalis, nightingales, finches, swallows. They say that they have unearthed an old text in which the author, comparing vulvas to swallows, says that he does not know which of them moves better or has the faster wing. However, The bird of Venus takes flight towards evening, they say they do not know what this means.

The golden fleece is one of the designations that have been given to the hairs that cover the pubis. As for the quests for the golden fleece to which certain ancient myths allude, the women say they know little of these. They say that the horseshoe which is a representation of the vulva has long been considered a lucky charm. They say that the most ancient figures depicting the vulva resemble horseshoes. They say that in fact it is in such a shape that they are represented on the walls of palaeolithic grottos.

The women say that the feminaries give pride of place to the symbols of the circle, the circumference, the ring, the O, the zero, the sphere. They say that this series of symbols has provided them with a guideline to decipher a collection of legends they have found in the library and which they have called the cycle of the Grail. These are to do with the quests to recover the Grail undertaken by a number of personages. They say it is impossible to mistake the symbolism of the Round Table that dominated their meetings. They say that, at the period when the texts were compiled, the quests for the Grail were singular unique attempts to describe the zero the circle the ring the spherical cup containing the blood. They say that, to judge by what they know about their subsequent history, the quests for the Grail were not successful, that they remained of the nature of a legend.

There are also legends in which young women having stolen fire carry it in their vulvas. There is the story of her who fell asleep for a hundred years from having wounded her finger with her spindle, the spindle being cited as the symbol of the clitoris. In connection with this story the women make many jokes about the awkwardness of the one who lacked the priceless guidance of a feminary. They say laughing that she must have been the freak spoken of elsewhere, she who, in place of a little pleasure-greedy tongue, had a poisonous sting. They say they do not understand why she was called the sleeping beauty.

Snow-White runs through the forest. Her feet catch in the roots of the trees, which make her trip repeatedly. The women say that the little girls know this story by heart. Rose-Red follows behind her, impelled to cry out while running. Snow-White says she is frightened. Snow-White running says, O my ancestors, I cast myself at your holy knees. Rose-Red laughs. She laughs so much that she falls, that she finally becomes angry. Shrieking with rage, Rose-Red pursues Snow-White with a stick, threatening to knock her down if she does not stop. Snow-White whiter than the silk of her tunic drops down at the foot of a tree. Then Rose-Red red as a peony or else red as a red rose marches furiously to and fro before her, striking the ground with her stick shouting, You haven't got any, you haven't got any, until eventually Snow-White asks, What is it that I have not got? the effect of which is to immobilize Rose-Red saying, Sacred ancestors, you haven't got any. Snow-White says that she has had enough, especially as she is no longer at all

OUGARIT EMERE BERTHA
JOAN ELIANA FEODISSIA
TORE SULEMNA AMARANTHIS
JIMINIA CRETESIPOLIS
VESPERA HEGEMONIA MAY
DORIS FORZITIA HEMANA

frightened and seizing hold of the stick she begins to run in all directions, she is seen striking out with all her might against the tree-trunks, lashing the yielding shrubs, striking the mossy roots. At a certain point she gives a great blow with the stick to Rose-Red asleep at the foot of an oak and resembling a stout root, pink as a pink rose.

The women say that they have found a very large number of terms to designate the vulva. They say they have kept several for their amusement. The majority have lost their meaning. If they refer to objects, these are objects now fallen into disuse, or else it is a matter of symbolic, geographical names. Not one of the women is found to be capable of deciphering them. On the other hand the comparisons present no problems. For example when the labia minora are compared to violets, or else the general appearance of the vulvas to sea-urchins or starfish. Periphrases such as genitals with double openings are cited in the feminaries. The texts also say that the vulvas resemble volutes, whorled shells. They are an eye embedded in eyelids that moves shines moistens. They are a mouth with its lips its tongue its pink palate. As well as rings and circles the feminaries give as symbols of the vulva triangles cut by a bisector ovals ellipses. Triangles have been designated in every alphabet by one or two letters. The ovals or ellipses may be stylized in the form of lozenges, or else in the shape of crescent moons, that is, ovals divided in two. These are the same symbols as the oval rings, settings surrounding stones of every colour. According to the feminaries rings are contemporaneous with such expressions as jewels treasures gems to designate the vulva.

The women say that it may be that the feminaries have fulfilled their function. They say they have no means of knowing. They say that thoroughly indoctrinated as they are with ancient texts no longer to hand, these seem to them outdated. All they can do to avoid being encumbered with useless knowledge is to heap them up in the squares and set fire to them. That would be an excuse for celebrations.

Sometimes it rains on the orange green blue islands. Then a mist hangs over them without obscuring their colours. The air one inhales is opaque and damp. One's lungs are like sponges that have imbibed water. The sharks swallow the necklaces that are thrown overboard to be got rid of, the strings of glassware, the opalescent baubles. A few stay stuck in the teeth of some shark that rolls over and over to free itself of them. One may glimpse its white belly. An equatorial vegetation is visible on the banks. The trees are all near the sea. They are bananas arengas oreodoxas euterpas arecas latanias caryotas elaeis. Except they are the green oaks of Scotland. There is no shelter the length of the beaches, there is no bay, there is no port. The islands are surrounded by a fringe of cerulean blue sea. The women stand, as it may be, on the bridge of the boat. Marie-Agnes Smyrne vomits the forty-seven oranges she swallowed whole for a bet. They fall from her mouth one by one, strings of saliva accompany them. At a certain point the ships' sirens are heard.

At each of their advances the women utter a brief cry. When they halt, their voices have long modulations. They move after the fashion of kangaroos, legs together which they bend to make their leap. Sometimes they spin on themselves like tops, heads in arms. It is during this movement that they exhale a perfume of arum lily verbena which spreads instantly through the surrounding space. The perfume differs according to the speed of their rotation. It disintegrates passing through various tonalities. Then it smells of mignonette lilac gardenia or else sweet-pea convulvulus nasturtium. It smells of warm rose-petals lychee currants. It smells of leaves decaying in the earth, the corpses of birds. When night falls they emerge from their furs to go to bed. They arrange them in the shape of bags, they hang them from the branches of trees and slip inside. Their colony is seen to cover the trees, as far as eye can reach, with great fur bundles.

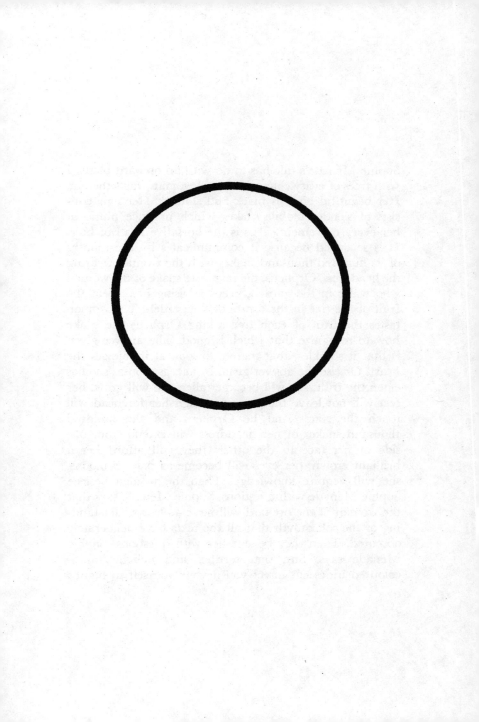

Sophie Ménade's tale has to do with an orchard planted
with trees of every colour. A naked woman walks therein.
Her beautiful body is black and shining. Her hair consists of slender mobile snakes which produce music at
her every movement. This is the hortative head of hair.
It is so called because it communicates by the mouths
of its hundred thousand snakes with the woman wearing
the headdress. Orpheus, the favourite snake of the woman
who walks in the garden, keeps advising her to eat the
fruit of the tree in the centre of the garden. The woman
tastes the fruit of each tree asking Orpheus the snake
how to recognize that which is good. The answer given
is that it sparkles, that merely to look at it rejoices the
heart. Or else the answer given is that, as soon as she has
eaten the fruit, she will become taller, she will grow, her
feet will not leave the ground though her forehead will
touch the stars. And he Orpheus and the hundred
thousand snakes of her headdress will extend from one
side of her face to the other, they will afford her a
brilliant crown, her eyes will become as pale as moons,
she will acquire knowledge. Then the women besiege
Sophie Ménade with questions. Sophie Ménade says that
the woman of the orchard will have a clear understanding of the solar myth that all the texts have deliberately
obscured. Then they besiege her with questions. Sophie
Ménade says, Sun that terrifies and delights/multi-
coloured iridescent insect you devour yourself in night's

memory/blazing genital/the circle is your symbol/you exist from all eternity/you will exist for all eternity. At these words the women begin to dance, stamping the ground with their feet. They begin a round dance, clapping their hands, giving voice to a song from which no coherent phrase emerges.

The women say that even without the feminaries they can recall the time when, as was typical of them, they made war. They say that all they need do is to invent terms that describe themselves without conventional references to herbals or bestiaries. They say that this can be done without pretension. They say that what they must stress above all is their strength and their courage.

The great register is laid open on the table. Every now and again one of them approaches and writes something therein. It is difficult to inspect it because it is rarely available. Even then it is useless to open it at the first page and search for any sequence. One may take it at random and find something one is interested in. This may be very little. Diverse as the writings are they all have a common feature. Not a moment passes without

one of the women approaching to write something therein. Or else a reading aloud of some passage takes place.
It may also happen that the reading occurs without any
audience, save for a fly that bothers the reader by settling
on her temple.

Sometimes Philomèle Sarte sings squatting on her heels,
swaying her bust forwards and backwards rocking from
right to left. Should she cease singing she falls forward,
face to the ground, or sideways, her cheek striking the
ground, her legs folding like a gun-dog's. Then she sings
on without a break. When her eyes close from fatigue
two of the women carry her to a bed or else on to the
grass in the sun and she falls asleep there.

Hélène Myre passes among the group with transparent
trays. Voices, murmurs are heard. From the orangery
there come the discordant sounds of a cartolo. Many of
the women blow a trumpet and wander running through
the avenues. Meanwhile Hélène Myre in passing offers
glasses of differently coloured syrups. If she is asked
what the blue or red liquid is she replies that the liquid
is the same whatever its colour, syrupy and sugary,

54

ROSAMUND ADELE EDME
DEBORAH OSMENA GALLIA
EDVOKIA ABIGAIL LAMIA
ESTEVA TIMARETA SAUGE
LEUCOTHEA ARLETTE MERE
PASIPHAË CARRIE AUDREY

fingers dipped in it are sticky and coloured. In this connection someone says jokingly, tell me your colour and I will tell you who you are. From the branches of the trees fall shooting stars which change from blue to red to orange and abruptly go out. Round lanterns are hung from the wire on which the fans of the fruit-trees are horizontally trained. At a certain point those suspended from the arches of the rose avenue catch fire, the light they shed fades, slowly disappears.

Their eyes, stuck to a shred of skin, are hidden in their long locks. When they toss their heads to shake some wisp off their cheeks or else when they bend forward, their eyes are visible rolling gleaming bluish haloed by the white of the agate-round cornea. They put their hands there only to tidy themselves, when they comb their hair strand by strand. Then each eye, touched, closes its lids, like a firefly going out. When they bound in the meadows holding each other by the hand, it seems as if there were hundreds of great pearls in their hair sparkling in the sun. If they begin to weep they are enclosed from head to foot in their falling tears. Through the light small rainbows halo them and make them glitter.

It is an animal without head or tail that resembles a top. It spins on itself without uttering a sound. Sometimes it is covered with scales, at others it is covered with feathers. No one knows how it moves. It is not seen to advance or retreat or move sideways as crabs do. All of a sudden it is there. It may emit a faint smell of aconite of incense or else smell unpleasantly of garlic or carnation. In the houses it stands in the centre of the rooms, ceaselessly spinning on itself. If it is forced to go away it suddenly appears again. Its eyes and mouth are at the level of the ground. They are invisible. It is possible that it makes use of them during its gyrations. It has no known cry. It is called the julep because it seems to have a predilection for rosewater. The little girls try to tame the juleps. They put them on a leash to drag them behind them. But even pulling with all their might they cannot succeed in making the juleps budge. They remain fixed to the point where they were seen to appear. They seem fixed to the ground by a species of magnetism.

The women say that they perceive their bodies in their entirety. They say that they do not favour any of its parts on the grounds that it was formerly a forbidden object. They say that they do not want to become prisoners of their own ideology. They say that they did not garner and develop the symbols that were necessary to them at an earlier period to demonstrate their strength.

For example they do not compare the vulvas to the sun moon stars. They do not say that the vulvas are like black suns in the shining night.

In a high wind the leaves fall from the trees. They go on to gather them in bread baskets. Some, scarcely touched, rot. They are scattered in the fields in the woods. In the baskets there are leaves of chestnut hornbeam maple clove guaiac copal oak mandarine willow copper-beech elm plane terebinth latania myrtle. Tébaïre Jade scatters them in the room crying, Friends do not let your imagination deceive you. You compare yourselves privately to the fruits of the chestnut cloves mandarines green oranges but you are fruits only in appearance. Like the leaves you fly away at the slightest breeze, beautiful strong light subtle and prompt of understanding as you are. Beware of dispersal. Remain united like the characters in a book. Do not abandon the collectivity. The women are seated on the piles of leaves holding hands watching the clouds that pass outside.

They play a game. It is performed on an enormous parade-ground. The ground is divided into zones corresponding to the colours of the spectrum. There are a hundred and fifty violet hoops a hundred and fifty indigo

METTE KHADIOTA MICHAELA
PHANO HUGUETTE LELIA
SIDONIA OMAYA MERNEITH
INIBRINA WUANG-QIANG
ASPASIA HANNAH LETITIA
NORA BENOITE RADEGONDE

hoops a hundred and fifty blue hoops a hundred and fifty green hoops a hundred and fifty yellow hoops a hundred and fifty orange hoops a hundred and fifty red hoops. The teams consist of seventy-five persons each, arranged on either side of the midline of the parade-ground. Each team has equal strips of violet indigo blue green yellow orange red territory. A machine situated at the centre of the parade-ground ejects the hoops one after the other at a fast pace. They rise vertically above the heads of the players. They rotate on themselves. At the same time they describe a vast circle which continually increases, due to the momentum imparted to them by the machine. The path of their movements would be an immense spiral. The women playing must catch the hoops without leaving the coloured zones allotted to them. Very soon there is an indescribable tumult of bodies jostling each other in the attempt to take hold of the same hoop or to withdraw from the confusion.

The bearers of fables are very welcome. A party is given in their honour. Tables are set up in the conservatories, in the orangeries. The drinks are mixed with narcotics, there are belladonna henbane nightshade datura in the wines in the spirits. There are also aphrodisiacs hashish opium. The drinkers are placid to begin with. Through the open doors they are visible stretched out on the divans, half asleep, or lying in the grass on the lawns. Later on they are seized with delirium. Some play an instrument and sing in part of the gardens, tears run down their cheeks, eventually sobs interrupt their singing. Others dance tangling their hair and stamping the ground with their feet with all their might. Around the tables, under the influence of the drugs, they engage in discourses which pile up paradoxes absurdities logomachies fallacies sophistries. At a certain point someone challenges the speakers, calling a halt, demanding reasoning devoid of error. Then the women all fall silent and go to sleep.

They do not say that vulvas with their elliptical shape are to be compared to suns, planets, innumerable galaxies. They do not say that gyratory movements are like vulvas. They do not say that the vulva is the primal form which as such describes the world in all its extent, in all its movement. They do not in their discourses create conventional figures derived from these symbols.

They weep, lying down or seated apart. The frost solidifies their tears which shine and sparkle on their cheeks. They weep, their sobs rack their bodies, they can be seen rolling in the snow. There are places where the wind blows white powdery clouds into their faces. Their cries moans lamentations do not rise from the depths. They might just as well be dumb. They do not bring their stiffened hands to their cheeks or their mouths to arrest the flow of blood from their gums. The icy *cirque* where they stand reflects all the sun's rays. The waves of light seem to detach themselves from the ground, to rise like flames, to quiver, to turn from red to orange-yellow or from pink to violet. It is like a volcanic crater that burns ready to overwhelm them.

Drunk, the women say they are drunk. Great fields of scarlet poppies have been trampled underfoot. Their heads, their torn petals hang loosely or lie in confusion on the ground. Not a drop of dew is visible on the flowers. The women dance. They hold each other round the neck and let themselves fall to the ground, lips black, eyes starting. They say they are drunk. Their arms and legs are bare. Their loosened hair hides their cheeks, then, flung back, reveals shining eyes, lips parted in song.

One must not run. One must walk patiently counting the number of one's steps. If one makes no mistake, if

ISADORA VI-SEUM JEZEBEL
ODILE ZUBAÏDA DINARZADE
GISELLE MARY CANDRA SITA
CELIMENA ASTRID MARLENE
CLEO LYSISTRATA ZENEIDA
EMON CLORINDA MESSALINA

one turns to the left at just the right moment, one will not touch the tree sticky with honey with one's outstretched arms. At this stage of the march one must interrupt the calculations and begin again at zero. If one makes no mistake in the calculations, if one jumps with feet together at just the right moment, one will not fall into the snake-pit. At this stage of the march one must interrupt the calculations and begin again at zero. If one makes no mistake in the calculations, if one bends down at just the right moment, one will not be caught in the jaws of the trap. At this stage of the march one must interrupt the calculations and begin again at zero. If one makes no mistake in the calculations and if one cries Sara Magre at just the right moment, one will fall into the arms of the incomparable, the gigantic, the wise Sara.

Six of the women are none too many to hold her. Her mouth is open. Inarticulate words and cries are heard. She stamps the ground with her feet. She twists her arms to free them from the grip, she shakes her head in every direction. At a given moment she lets herself fall to the ground, she strikes the ground with her arms, she rolls about shrieking. Her mouth seizes the earth and spits it out. Her gums bleed. Words like death blood blood burn death war war war are heard. Then she tears her garments and bangs her head on the ground until she falls silent, done for. Four of the women carry her, singing, Behind my eyelids/the dream has not reached my soul/ whether I sleep or wake/there is no rest.

To greet the messengers they go beneath the great oak. In the greatest heat it casts a cool shade. They are seated in a circle. They speak or doze. Sometimes no messenger arrives. Then they rise and shaking out their clothes they disperse and are lost to sight in the branching avenues.

Sometimes the women may chance to talk together about the latest fable that has been told them. For example Diane Ebèle tells Aimée Dionis the fable of Koue Feï which is about a young girl who pursues the sun. She is constantly on the point of catching it. To escape her, the sun plunges into the sea. Koue Feï then starts to swim after it. Thus she traverses the entire ocean. She comes up to it just when it is leaving the water, about to escape her again. Hastily Koue Feï jumps into the sun and instals herself within it. She makes it sway from side to side in its course, several stars fall because of this. But Koue Feï has managed to sit inside the sun. Now she controls its path. She can make it follow its orbit faster or slower as she wishes. That is why, in order to have good weather when they leave for the fishing, the two little girls address themselves to Koue Feï, mistress of the sun, so that she may pause for a while above the sea.

c

The weather-vanes are arranged next to each other on the hill. The metal blades that rotate round the shafts are painted green blue red white yellow black. Each blade is surrounded by long fine fringes which are borne up by the wind. None of the weather-vanes point in the same direction. Some turn at full speed. The white ones in their movements retain the light of the sun. Like mirrors they reflect its flashes.

In speaking of their genitals the women do not employ hyperboles metaphors, they do not proceed sequentially or by gradation. They do not recite long litanies, whose refrain is an unending imprecation. They do not strive to multiply the intervals so that in sum they signify a deliberate lapse. They say that all these forms denote an outworn language. They say everything must begin over again. They say that a great wind is sweeping the earth. They say that the sun is about to rise.

DIONE INEZ HESIONE ELIZA
VICTORIA OTHYS DAMHURACI
ASHMOUNIGAL NEPHTYS CIRCE
DORA DENISE CAMILLA BELLA
CHRISTINA GERMANICA LAN-ZI
SIMONA HEGET ZONA DRAGA

They look at the coloured picture on the screen. The façade of pink bricks glitters in the frost. Some rays of the rising sun strike it glancingly, setting the window-panes ablaze. On a pile of branches with dried-up leaves there are thrown the drooping faded flower-heads of roses marguerites anemones. The next picture shows the sky where not a bird passes, the fountain in front of the house where the water does not flow. Later they look at the four great trimmed plane-trees and the regular area they bound, almost a square, made of a well-shorn meadow. The house can be glimpsed again between the four trees. The pediment is a narrow triangle. The shutters are entirely of wood. The main door can be seen to be slightly ajar. The red tiles of the entrance hall are visible.

The women stand by the lake shore. Their words and their songs blend into a sonorous whole that is reflected by the flat surface from the other side. The opaque bell-jars of the water-spiders make holes here and there in the water. When daylight fades the reflections of the trees are enormous. The ephemerides dart forward at water-level. Thousands of flat-bellied soldier-flies lie still on the irises the water-lilies the great lilies. The women study their reflections. They are like an army of giantesses. The outlines of their garments are interrupted. The green and red colours that compose them make unquiet splashes that are not motionless, that coalesce and re-disintegrate. When one looks around it is apparent that the reflections are reproduced in the series of eighteen lakes, all identical, all distorted.

Their peregrinations are cyclical and circular. Whatever the itinerary, whatever point of departure they choose, they end up at the same place. The paths are parallel, equidistant, narrower and narrower as they approach the centre of the figure. If they follow the path from the interior to the exterior they must traverse the widest of the circles before finding the cross-passage that leads them to the centre. The system is closed. No radius starting from the centre allows of any expansion or of breaking through. At the same time it is without limit, the juxta-position of the increasingly widening circles configures every possible revolution. It is virtually that infinite sphere whose centre is everywhere, circumference no-where.

One of the women relates the death of Adèle Donge and how the embalming of her body was carried out. The story tells how she is placed on a trestle table. The intestines are withdrawn through the open belly. The abdomen emptied of its organs is washed with water to which sulphuric acid has been added. Then it is dried. Various substances are introduced, ground mint benzoin sage styrax mixed with formalin phenol permanganate hydrogen peroxide. The separated layers and membranes have to be reunited, they must be sewn together. The head is emptied of the brain after the cranium has been drilled using a trephine. Balsamatic desiccative antiseptic substances are introduced into the cranial cavity. The viscera are preserved like precious materials in large glass jars that bear inscriptions. They ignore the brain. They abandon it carelessly on some piece of furniture. A domestic animal might seize and devour it. The women yawn at this account or else they applaud without much enthusiasm.

Now they are marching through a field of tall flowers. The orange-yellow tufts bend over above their heads. When the women stumble against the stalks pollen falls from the shaken pistils in great quantity. The giant flower is a stem whose extremity is rolled up on itself, it is whorled, it copies the shape of a bishop's crozier. The hermaphrodis is a flower that gives off an overpowering perfume. Among the marchers some can no longer keep up. They fall on their knees, they let themselves sink to the ground, head dropping, body like a gun-dog's. Or else they writhe with their arms, they cry out, they throw themselves face down as if seized with madness. They

JILL STEPHANIE CYDIPPA
OLEA ALBERTINE DELMIRA
ANDREA SOPHONISBE ALBA
CLELIA TAI-REN BUTHAYNA
JEPHTHA HOLAA BLANDINA
ATIKA NAUNAME CHRYSEIS

advance into the forest, between the stiff woody stems, faces caught by the sun, covered by the pollen that escapes continually from the invisible stamens.

The story told by Emily Norton takes place at a time when every detail of a birth is ceremoniously regulated. When the child is born the midwife begins to utter cries like women who fight in battle. This means that the mother has conquered as a warrior and that she has captured a child. The women look over Emily Norton's shoulder at the effigies of women with mouths wide open, screaming, squatting, the child's head between their thighs.

They say that at the point they have reached they must examine the principle that has guided them. They say it is not for them to exhaust their strength in symbols. They say henceforward what they are is not subject to compromise. They say they must now stop exalting the vulva. They say that they must break the last bond that binds them to a dead culture. They say that any symbol that exalts the fragmented body is transient, must disappear. Thus it was formerly. They, the women, the integrity of the body their first principle, advance marching together into another world.

Things being in this state, they summon the trades. Distaffs looms rollers shuttles combs point-paper presses cams cloth toiles cashmere twill calico crepe chintz satin spools of thread sewing-machines typewriters reams of paper stenographers' pads ink-bottles knitting-needles ironing-boards machine-tools spinners bobbin-winders staplers assembly-lines tweezers blow-lamps soldering-irons bonders yarn for braiding for twisting knitting-machines cauldrons great wooden tubs stew-pans sauce pans plates stoves brooms of every bristle vacuum-cleaners washing-machines brushes et cetera. They heap them on to an immense pyre to which they set fire, blowing up everything that will not burn. Then, starting to dance round it, they clap their hands, they shout obscene phrases, they cut their hair or let it down. When the fire has burnt down, when they are sated with setting off explosions, they collect the débris, the objects that are not consumed, those that have not melted down, those that have not disintegrated. They cover them with blue green red paint to reassemble them in grotesque grandiose abracadabrant compositions to which they give names.

The shape of my shield/is the white belly of a snake/ day and night I watch over your safety. Françoise Barthes reads out aloud from the great register the story of Trung Nhi and Trung Trac. Françoise Barthes says that it is about two young peasant women who always fought side by side. They died together after three years of war. They were to be seen shoulder to shoulder in the thick of the battle, conspicuous, embodiments of the sinews of the revolt against the powerful feudal armies. Both shields raised, black and white, those of Trung Nhi and Trung Trac stand out in the mêlées, ever close to one another, their lances directed towards the enemy. Françoise Barthes says that, whatever great battles the women may have waged or may wage, it is unthinkable ever to forget the two Trung sisters.

A shining black snake with carmine red rings lies coiled in the grass in the sun. Its body seems to be mineral, a sort of jet. If it is touched with the tip of a finger it barely stirs. It barely stirs even when it is picked up to be used as an ornament, when it is coiled lengthwise round the neck the chest the waist. Replaced on the ground it seems to go to sleep. In this connection someone recalls the existence of an ancient sect, the Ophidians, who used to worship snakes. She demonstrates one of their ritual gestures, one phase of which consists of kissing the snake. Then she puts her lips to the black scales.

ALIDA LUDWIGE OLINDA
WILHELMINA GASPARDE
REGINA MALVIDA DIOTIMA
MADELEINE PHENARETE IVY
RICARDA COSIMA NU-JIAO
LAURENTIA LABAN AMABLE

News has arrived from the assembly that is compiling the dictionary. The example proposed to illustrate the word hate has been rejected. It concerns a phrase of Anne-Louise Germaine, The women have transformed hate into energy and energy into hate. It has been adduced as a reason that the phrase contains an antithesis and therefore lacks precision. The bearer of these tidings, who is called Jeanne Sbire, is hissed. The women surround her jostle her insult her. Jeanne Sbire weeps hot tears, saying she cannot help it. Then the women get angry saying that an antithesis is indeed involved and why has it not been suppressed, retaining the first part of the phrase which alone has any meaning. Then they chant at the top of their voices the famous song which begins, Let a hundred flowers blossom, a hundred schools compete.

Great gatherings assemble at dawn when a blue light is still visible over the roofs of the houses. The voices are sonorous and clear. There is a great migration. In the caravanserais steaming cauldrons are placed on the tables, bowls are filled from ladles, are handed round. There is a strong smell of coffee. It is noticeable in the street. It passes through the open windows. Some of the women move forward slowly in little groups along the avenues, they drag their feet, their faces are heavy with sleep. Others wait, standing in the square, they can be seen yawning. The columns begin to march before day has yet broken. They are in uniform order. Their identical costume is tinged by the blue light of before dawn. The tramping is that of a troop that moves off, they fall into proper rank, they find their rhythm. Later the sun appears.

The women tell how the horses returned from Souame, grey, dirty, lame, riderless, walking slowly, pressed flank to flank. From time to time one of them lifts its head and shakes its mane. Not a neigh is heard. An unshod hoof scrapes the ground, turning over the pebbles. Some of the horses are wounded, the blood flows over their bellies. Or else they advance on three legs, the fourth is broken galled slashed. Those that still bear saddles have the stirrups banging against their flanks, ill-fastened. Most have lost them.

Someone speaks of the women who have gone as delegates to the opposing armies. These are young women who sit down decisively to parley. They wear the white costume of those who stand for peace. They make their way without a moment's rest to the places assigned to them. The saliva on their tongues is thick with the dust of travel. The armies are invisible. Once a route is decided on no heed is paid to the days the enterprise takes. They are on the march. If the sun appears they keep their eyes fixed on it. Or else they look at the moon and the stars. They do not know when they will be able to rest their limbs and sleep shielded from the light, eyes closed.

It is learned that in the world of the Four Powers the women have sustained casualties. Several hundred of them have had their legs broken. For the time being they must lie in small invalid carriages. Those seconded to their care push them along the streets of the town. It is they who wash them and keep them alive. A debate is held to decide what is best to be done. It is a matter of despatching small clandestine groups to sustain the morale of the dissidents. Thus the Front as a whole will be in permanent liaison with the world of the Four Powers. As well as information and orders, advice encouragement and exhortation will not be spared.

The women say that they have been given as equivalents the earth the sea tears that which is humid that which is black that which does not burn that which is negative those who surrender without a struggle. They say this

OURIKA AKAZOME CYPRIS
LEONTINE ANGELICA LIA
RODOGUNE JASMINE KALI
SIVAN-KI ZULMA CYANA
GALERIA HELLAN AIMATA
SAMARE JOSUE SAKANYA

is a concept which is the product of mechanistic reasoning. It deploys a series of terms which are systematically related to opposite terms. Its theses are so crass that the thought of them makes the women start laughing violently. They say they might just as well be compared with the sky the heavenly bodies in their general movement and disposition the galaxies the planets the stars the suns that which burns those who struggle bravely those who do not surrender. They joke on this subject, they say it is to fall between Scylla and Charybdis, to avoid one religious ideology only to adopt another, they say that both one and the other have this in common, that they are no longer valid.

They persuade Shu Ji to tell them the story of Nü Wa. Shu Ji relates how the mountain in Nü Wa's country crumbled, how the sky began to tilt to one side, how the earth began to sink. It is then that Nü Wa undertook to remedy this state of affairs. She is seen hewing rocks of every colour to repair the sky, cutting off the feet of a giant tortoise to set the world aright on the four cardinal points. Everything that lives in that country is in mortal danger because of the black dragon. Then Nü Wa wages a great battle against the dragon and eventually kills it. Shu Ji says that Nü Wa however has not yet reached the end of her difficulties. The waters that were released at the time of the cataclysm cover the earth. Thus it is that Nü Wa sets fire to all the reeds of her kingdom until, completely consumed, they absorb the water with their ashes.

In recalling that Lei Zu is she who discovered silk the manner in which she arrived at this outcome is not mentioned. It may have resulted from a series of observations she made herself. Or else some one of her followers may have bequeathed her the monopoly of this industry. Or perhaps the first success was obtained by a young peasant girl and Lei Zu learned of it. It may also be imagined that Lei Zu is an empress without followers and without pomp, that she has acquired by observation experimental knowledge of the bombyx. Indeed it is written that after having discovered the silkworm Lei Zu brought their cultivation and the manufacture of their silk to a fine art. As a first step Lei Zu discovers the material that can be extracted from the threadlike substance secreted by the bombyxes when they surround themselves with a cocoon. As a second step she realizes the need to produce artificially great concentrations of bombyxes. As a third step she determines the several operations essential for the production of silk thread : sorting the cocoons, asphyxiating the chrysalises, emptying the cocoons to obtain the raw silk, drawing the raw silk out into threads or else spinning it mechanically using a jenny furnished with spindles.

The women say that they could carry out great ceremonies of mourning. For example they could bewail the death of Julie. One of them asks if she has been strangled and if this was done with a violet material. Another says that she was publicly hanged on a gibbet, her feet protruding beyond her long tunic, her head shorn in sign of infamy. They say that perhaps she was decapitated, the neck being severed from the head and letting a wave of blood escape from the carotid. It may also be that she was broken alive on the wheel in the public square. To her who asks the nature of her crime they answer that it was identical with that of the woman of whom it is written that she saw that the tree of the garden was good to eat, tempting to see, and that it was the tree requisite for gaining understanding.

When there are no high trees beside the avenues thickets of willows birches apples bushes of box hedges or even very tall flowers, the eye can trace their extent in its entirety. In whatever part of the garden one may happen to be, one can ascertain by turning completely around the geometric forms that govern the network of figures. If the system is rigorous one can combine multiple itineraries. The limits and the proportions of the figures are related to a hypothetical infinity in the same way as the diverse series of numbers.

VASA FABIANA BELISSUNU
NEBKA MAUD ARETE MAAT
ATALANTA DIOMEDE URUK
OM FRANCOISE NAUSICAA
PUDUHEPA KUWATALLA
AGATHOCLEA BOZENA NADA

The two armies confront each other. The embattled women stand motionless, awaiting the order to move forward. In their hands they hold kites the colour of their army. One lot is red, the others are blue. The kites are stationary, aligned vertically above their heads. The trumpets are sounded. They attack. All at once there is a confusion of red and blue kites, of red and blue bodies. The kites collide violently. Some escape with a great rustling. A red kite is motionless over the sea. A combatant runs along the beach trying to gain possession of it. A band of blue kites escape towards the dunes, they are pursued by red kites. Laughter and singing are heard. Some of the women, deprived of their kites, are stretched out in the middle of the battlefield, bleeding.

The women incite with their laughs and shouts those who fight in the grass. They fight until they bring each other down. Their thighs, their knees, are seen in motion. Their strength is based on the firm seating of the trunk on the pelvis. They have straight backs that bend vigorously and are lissome at the loins. Later, stiffly erect, they march towards the hills. They find closed villages, stoutly walled. Then, addressing themselves to the walls, they ask which of them possesses the greatest strength.

The women say they have learned to rely on their own strength. They say they are aware of the force of their unity. They say, let those who call for a new language first learn violence. They say, let those who want to change the world first seize all the rifles. They say that they are starting from zero. They say that a new world is beginning.

To Hippolyta was sent the lion of the triple night. They say that it took three nights to engender a monster with a human face capable of overcoming the queen of the Amazons. The stern fight she had using bow and arrows, his desperate resistance when she dragged it far into the mountains so as not to jeopardize the life of her kin, they say they know nothing of these, that the story has not been written. They say that until that day the women had always been defeated.

The game consists of posing a series of questions, for example, Who says, I wish it, I order it, my will must take the place of reason? Or, Who must never act according to their will? Or else, Who is only an animal the colour of flowers? There are plenty of others such as,

Who must observe the three obediences and whose destiny is written in their anatomy? The answer to all the questions is the same. Then they begin to laugh ferociously slapping each other on the shoulders. Some of the women, lips parted, spit blood.

To sleep they enter the white cells. These are hollowed out in the rock-face by hundreds of thousands. Their concentric openings are tangential. The women travel there rapidly, at full speed in fact. Naked, their hair covering their shoulders, they choose their places as they climb. It is possible to lie down in the cell, which resembles an egg, a sarcophagus, an O in view of the shape of its aperture. Several can stay there together gesticulating, singing, sleeping. It is a place of privileged sanctuary though not sealed off. The isolation of one cell from another is such that, even if one bangs with all one's might against the ovoid wall, the sound of the blows is not perceived in the adjacent cell. When one is lying down in the cell it is impossible to discern the occupants of the other cells. Before the general retirement for the night confused murmurs of voices are heard, then, distinctly, the phrase, This order must be changed, forcefully repeated by thousands of voices.

ANACTORIA PSAPPHA LETO
OUBAOUÉ CHEA NINEGAL
IPHIS LYDIA GENEVIEVE
EUGENIA THEODORA WATI
NOUT BETTE HETEPHERES
GUDRUN VERONICA EMMA

The habitations are gem-studded multicoloured spherical. Some are transparent. Some float in the air and drift gently. Others are attached to dull steel pylons that look like stalks from a distance. The habitations are affixed at differing heights, their interposition varies. There is no symmetry in their arrangement. They are attached to the pylons at right angles by transverse shafts. The length of these shafts also varies. It is not possible at this distance to determine what allows the inhabitants to gain access to their houses. The pylons are very tall. Their metallic structures with their clean and precise outlines are seen against the horizon. The spheres are suspended from them by the hundred thousand. Between the spheres are seen moving clouds, the sun or the moon, the stars. When the wind gets up the spheres all begin to move at once, soundlessly. From every point on the plain the women march towards the town. They wear identical costumes. These consist of black trousers, flared below, narrow at the hips, and white tunics that confine the bust. They are bare-footed or else they wear light sandals. Several among them march singing long interminably modulated phrases in a high-pitched voice, for example, Cry, is there gold elsewhere more celestial/the wasps of bullets are not for me.

There are there Elsa Brauer Julie Brunèle Odile Roques Evelyne Sabir. They stand before the great gathering of women. Elsa Brauer strikes the cymbals one against the other when she stops speaking, while Julie Brunèle Odile Roques Evelyne Sabir accompany her with long rolls on their drums. Elsa Brauer says something like, There was a time when you were not a slave, remember that. You walked alone, full of laughter, you bathed bare-bellied. You say you have lost all recollection of it, remember. The wild roses flower in the woods. Your hand is torn on the bushes gathering the mulberries and strawberries you refresh yourself with. You run to catch the young hares that you flay with stones from the rocks to cut them up and eat all hot and bleeding. You know how to avoid meeting a bear on the track. You know the winter fear when you hear the wolves gathering. But you can remain seated for hours in the tree-tops to await morning. You say there are no words to describe this time, you say it does not exist. But remember. Make an effort to remember. Or, failing that, invent.

They speak together of the threat they have constituted towards authority, they tell how they were burned on pyres to prevent them from assembling in future. They were able to command tempests, to sink fleets, to destroy armies. They have been mistresses of poisons, of the winds, of the will. They were able to exercise their powers at will and to transform all kinds of persons into mere animals, geese pigs birds turtles. They have ruled over life and death. Their conjoint power has menaced hierarchies systems of government authorities. Their knowledge has competed successfully with the official knowledge to which they had no access, it has challenged it, found it wanting, threatened it, made it appear inefficacious. No police were powerful enough to track them down, no paid informer so opportunist, no torture so brutal, no army so overwhelming as to attack them one by one and destroy them. Then they chant the famous song that begins, Despite all the evils they wished to crush me with/I remain as steady as the three-legged cauldron.

The progression continues simultaneously with the completion of the cycle. But that is to say too much or too little. The women say that, to complete a cycle, a series of brilliant deeds or extraordinary and baleful events is required. Charlotte Bernard says that they are not concerned. Emmanuela Chartre says that it is no longer done to marvel at this kind of cycle. Marie Serge says that in any case the cycle may relate to myth and may not mention acts that have any semblance of reality. Flaminie Pougens says that for the women to be wholly engaged it is necessary to invent these. Then they laugh and fall backward from force of laughing. All are infected. A noise rises like the rolling of drums under a vault. The bricks of the ceiling fall one by one, uncovering through the openings the gilded panelling of lofty rooms. The stones of the mosaics fly out, the glass panes clatter down, there are shafts of blue red orange mauve.

NU-JUAN BAHISSAT VLADIA
EMILY MEROPE DOMITIA
ANNABEL SELMA MUMTAZ
NUR-JAMAN OUADA ARTHIS
ARIANA LEONTINE CAROL
GURINNO GONGYLA ARIGNOTA

The laughter does not lessen. The women pick up the bricks and using them as missiles they bombard the statues that remain standing in the midst of the disorder. They set about bringing down the remaining stones. There is a terrible clash of stone against stone. They evacuate those among them who are injured. The systematic destruction of the building is carried through by the women in the midst of a storm of cries shouts, while the laughter continues, spreads, becomes general. It comes to an end only when nothing remains of the building but stones on stones. Then they lie down and fall asleep.

In Hélène Fourcade's story, Trieu has deployed her troops at daybreak. She is seated motionless on a white elephant. One by one the women, the captains, come to salute her. They hold out their bare hands before her, palms open towards the sky in token of loyalty. Then each of the armies marches past, heads turned towards the motionless Trieu. The last units execute a wheeling movement on the spot. The garments of the combatants are blue, without ornament. Trieu is dressed in red. When all are still and have placed their weapons at their feet Trieu removes the silk band that binds her head. Her black hair uncoils and falls abruptly over her shoulders. Then the combatants utter a great cry chanting the song, May the rice-fields rot/for those who invade them/day and night/we fight without truce. They say that it is better to die than to live as slaves. At this point Trieu starts forward at the head of a detachment.

They say that they leap like the young horses beside the Eurotas. Stamping the ground they speed their movements. They shake their hair like the bacchantes who love to agitate their thyrsi. They say, quickly now, fasten your floating hair with a bandeau and stamp the ground. Stamp it like a doe, beat out the rhythm needed for the dance, homage to warlike Minerva, the warrior, bravest of the goddesses. Begin the dance, step forward lightly, move in a circle, hold each other by the hand, let everyone observe the rhythm of the dance. Spring forward lightly. The ring of dancers must revolve so that their glance lights everywhere.

They say that they foster disorder in all its forms. Confusion troubles violent debates disarray upsets disturbances incoherences irregularities divergences complications disagreements discords clashes polemics discussions contentions brawls disputes conflicts routs débâcles cataclysms disturbances quarrels agitation turbulence conflagrations chaos anarchy.

93

The women say that they have a concern for strategy and tactics. They say that the massive armies that comprise divisions corps regiments sections companies are ineffectual. Their exercises consist of manoeuvres marches guards patrols. These afford no real practice for combat. They say that they do not prepare for combat. They say that in these armies the handling of weapons is not taught efficiently. They say that such armies are institutions. One refers to their barracks their posts their garrisons. One speaks of their transport their engineers their artillery their infantry their general staff. In this context strategy consists of making plans of campaign operational tactics of advance and retreat. Thus strategy is equivalent to tactics, both being short-term. They say that with this concept of war weapons are difficult to deploy, effectives cannot adapt to every situation, most of the time they fight over unfamiliar ground. They say that they are not noted for audacity. They say that they cannot fight with precision, they retreat or advance according to plans whose tactics and strategy are beyond them. They say that these armies are not formidable, their effectives being conscript, participation not being voluntary.

Their favourite weapons are portable. They consist of rocket-launchers which they carry on the shoulder. The shoulder serves as a support for firing. It is possible to run and change position extremely quickly without loss of fire-power. There is every kind of rifle. There are machine-guns and rocket-launchers. There are traps with jaws in ditches pitfalls hollows lined with rows of slicing bamboo-blades driven in as stakes. The manoeuvres are raids ambushes surprise attacks followed by a rapid retreat. The objective is not to gain ground but to destroy the greatest number of the enemy to annihilate his armament to compel him to move blindly never to grant him the initiative in engagements to harass him without pause. Using such tactics, to put an enemy out of action without killing him is to immobilize several individuals, the one who is wounded and those who bring aid, it is the best way to sow disarray.

The women say that, with the world full of noise, they see themselves as already in possession of the industrial complexes. They are in the factories aerodromes radio stations. They have control of communications. They have taken possession of aeronautical electronic ballistic data-processing factories. They are in the foundries tall furnaces navy yards arsenals refineries distilleries. They have taken possession of pumps presses levers rolling-mills winches pullies cranes turbines pneumatic drills arcs

blow-lamps. They say that they envisage themselves acting with strength and happiness. They say that they hear themselves shout and sing, Let the sun shine/the world is ours.

Look at him, this cripple, who hides his calves as best he can. Look at his timid springless gait. In his cities it is easy to do him violence. You lie in wait for him at a street-corner one night. He thinks you are beckoning to him. You profit by this to take him by surprise, he hasn't even the reflex to cry out. Ambushed in his towns you chase him, you lay hands on him, you capture him, you surprise him shouting with all your might.

The women say that they could not eat hare veal or fowl, they say that they could not eat animals, but man, yes, they may. He says to them throwing his head back with pride, poor wretches of women, if you eat him who will go to work in the fields, who will produce food consumer goods, who will make the aeroplanes, who will pilot them, who will provide the spermatozoa, who will write the books, who in fact will govern? Then the women laugh, baring their teeth to the fullest extent.

He begins to cry. And they say no, they could not eat the lion dog puma lamb giraffe mouse ladybird blackbird rabbit-stew. They say, look at this cripple who hides his calves as best he can. They say that he is ideal quarry. They say they must eat to live. He persists in saying that man is devoid of fangs claws trunk legs for running. He persists in saying, why attack such a defenceless creature?

They say that most of the men are lying down. They are not all dead. They sleep. The women say of themselves that they leap like young horses on the banks of the Eurotas. Stamping the ground, they speed their movements. They shake their hair like the bacchantes who love to agitate their thyrsi. They say, quickly now, fasten your floating hair with a bandeau and stamp the ground. Stamp it like a doe, beat out the rhythm needed for the dance, homage to warlike Minerva, the warrior, bravest of the goddesses. Begin the dance. Step forward lightly, move in a circle, hold each other by the hand, let everyone observe the rhythm of the dance. Spring forward lightly. The ring of dancers must revolve so that their glance lights everywhere. They say, It is a great error to imagine that I, a woman, would speak violence against men. But we must, as something quite new, begin the round dance stamping the feet in time against the ground. They say, rise slowly twice clapping your hands. Stamp the ground in time, O women. Now turn to the other side. Let the foot move in rhythm.

The women make warlike gestures, approaching and retreating, dancing with their hands and feet. Some hold bamboo poles sorghum stems wooden batons the long ones representing lances and great halberds, the short ones double-edged swords or ordinary sabres. Dispersing by gates and paths they jostle each other impetuously. Their violence is extreme. They crash into each other with bravura. No one can restrain them. Each time these exercises take place several dozen of them are needed so that they may play together thus.

They stand on the ramparts, faces covered with a shining powder. They can be seen all round the town, singing together a kind of mourning song. The male besiegers are near the walls, indecisive. Then the women, at a signal, uttering a terrible cry, suddenly rip off the upper part of their garments, uncovering their naked gleaming breasts. The men, the enemy, begin to discuss what they unanimously regard as a gesture of submission. They send ambassadors to treat for the gates to be opened. Three of their number fall struck down by stones as soon as they are within range. The entire army hurls itself against the walls, with battering-rams flame-throwers guns scaling-ladders. A great tumult rises. The besiegers utter cries of rage. The women, modulating their voices into a stridency that distresses the ear, withstand the siege, one by one, with arrows stones burning pitch, not quitting their positions except to bring aid to someone or to replace a dead woman. Within, long processions come and go, some bringing pitch, others water to extinguish the fires. The combatants are visible above the wall, singing without pause, their mouths wide open over white teeth. Their cheeks still glow in their blackened faces. Some laugh out loud and manifest their aggressiveness by thrusting their bare breasts forward brutally.

The women say, the men have kept you at a distance, they have supported you, they have put you on a pedestal, constructed with an essential difference. They say, men in their way have adored you like a goddess or else burned you at their stakes or else relegated you to their service in their back-yards. They say, so doing they have always in their speech dragged you in the dirt. They say, in speaking they have possessed violated taken subdued

OEDIPA PERNETTA MERCY
GERMAINE DAPHNE CYNTHIA
SHIRLEY NIOBE HARRIET
ROXANA CAROLINE HULDA
DAISY PRAHOMIRA MANYE
FLORENCE SHADTAR ASTA

humiliated you to their hearts' content. They say, oddly enough what they have exalted in their words as an essential difference is a biological variation. They say, they have described you as they described the races they called inferior. They say, yes, these are the same domineering oppressors, the same masters who have said that negroes and women do not have a heart spleen liver in the same place as their own, that difference of sex difference of colour signify inferiority, their own right to domination and appropriation. They say, yes, these are the same domineering oppressors who have written of negroes and women that they are universally cheats hypocrites tricksters liars shallow greedy faint-hearted, that their thinking is intuitive and illogical, that nature is what speaks most loudly in them, et cetera. They say, yes, these are the same domineering oppressors who sleep crouched over their money-bags to protect their wealth and who tremble with fear when night comes.

The women are on their cavorting continually rearing horses. They proceed without orders to meet the enemy army. They have painted their faces and legs in bright colours. The cries they utter are so terrifying that many of their adversaries drop their weapons, running straight before them stopping their ears. The women are on the ridges that command the pass. In this strategic position which is all to their advantage they draw their bows and fire thousands of arrows. Then the army breaks ranks.

The men all begin to run in the greatest confusion, some go towards the exit from the pass, others try to retrace their steps. They jostle and collide with each other as they flee, they stumble over the bodies of the dead and wounded. Orders are no longer heard. Cries of despair panic shrieks of pain are heard. Many throw down their swords that hamper them in flight. Some climb on the hills making signs of surrender, they are soon slaughtered. When the bottom of the valley has become a charnel-house the women brandish their bows above their heads, they utter shouts of victory, they chant a song of death in which these words are heard, Vulture with the bald head/brother of the dead/vulture perform your office/ with the corpses I offer you/receive also this vow/never shall my arrow be planted in your eyes.

The Ophidian women the Odonates the Oögones the Odoacres the Olynthians the Oöliths the Omphales the women of Ormur of Orphise the Oriennes have massed and gone over to the attack. The convoys that follow them bring arms victuals clothes. They travel at night, rejoining the armies at daybreak when they withdraw after having given battle. Their most formidable weapon is the ospah. They hold it in position above their heads and rotate it at full speed by twirling the right arm as with a lasso that one spins before one or like the leather thong with bolos attached that one throws round the legs of wild horses to trip them. The ospah is invisible so long as it is not in action. When it is manipulated during battle it materializes as a green circle which crackles and emits odours. Thus the women, making it move at full speed in a given direction, create with the ospah a zone of death. No ray, no shot, no fulguration are seen to emanate from the ospah. The coalescence of the O's is produced by the desperate combatants, full of courage audacious tough and unyielding.

The little girls have laid down their rifles. They advance into the sea and plunge into it, the sweat running down their necks, under their armpits, along their backs. Or else, stretched out in the sun, they talk very loudly. Some, unable to stay still, jump in the sand and jostle each other. One of them, quite naked, with tresses of hair over each shoulder, standing in front of a group, recites at a stretch, Is the finest thing on the dark earth really a group of horsemen whose horses go at a trot or a troop of infantry stamping the ground? Is the finest thing really a squadron of ships side by side? Anactoria Kypris Savé have a bearing a grace a radiant brightness of countenance that are pleasanter to see than all the chariots of the Lydians and their warriors charging in their armour. Then the women applaud.

VINCENTA CLOTILDA NICOLA
SUKAINA XU-HU ANACHORA
OLYMPA DELPHINA LUCRETIA
ROLANDA VIOLA BERNARDA
PHUONG PLANCINE CLORINDA
BAO-SI PULCHERIA AUGUSTA

The women say that men put all their pride in their tail.
They mock them, they say that the men would like a
long tail but that they would run away whining as soon
as they stepped on it. The women guffaw and begin to
imitate some ridiculous animal that has difficulty in getting about. When they have a prisoner they strip him
and make him run through the streets crying, it is your
rod/cane/staff/wand/peg skewer/staff of lead. Sometimes the subject has a fine body broadened at the hips
with honeyed skin and muscles not showing. Then they
take him by the hand and caress him to make him forget
all their bad treatment.

The women say, you are really a slave if ever there was
one. Men have made what differentiates them from you
the sign of domination and possession. They say, you will
never be numerous enough to spit on their phallus, you
will never be sufficiently determined to stop speaking
their language, to burn their currency their effigies their
works of art their symbols. They say, men have foreseen
everything, they have christened your revolt in advance
a slave revolt, a revolt against nature, they call it revolt

when you want to appropriate what is theirs, the phallus. The women say, I refuse henceforward to speak this language, I refuse to mumble after them the words lack of penis lack of money lack of insignia lack of name. I refuse to pronounce the names of possession and non-possession. They say, If I take over the world, let it be to dispossess myself of it immediately, let it be to forge new links between myself and the world.

The women advance side by side in a geometric order of progress. The interval of a few yards that they maintain between them is invisible at a distance. The first rank that advances covers the width of the plain. The tall buildings crumble like card houses at their passage emitting a thick dust over which they march. The second rank of combatants marches some hundred yards behind the first, covering like that one the whole width of the plain. They are followed by another rank at the same distance, by yet another, until one can no longer distinguish their outlines as they blend with the horizon.

As far as eye can see there is no house standing. The combatants carry in both hands a small sphere which has a crateriform part that is directed in front of them at the level of their belts. At every obstacle that presents itself to their progress they project a beam of convergent rays the power of whose impact is signalled by a murky flash, a brief glare, which ensures that any object that may be in the field of the rays is instantly destroyed. They wear garments all of one piece, made of a kind of metal. Their faces, intermittently lit up by the spheres and their rays, resemble great insect heads with antennae and stalked eyes.

The women await their emissaries on their doorsteps, a smile on their lips. They have let down their hair, they have assumed the military costume that leaves the body free in its movements. Within the houses they have poured out the dishwater and scattered the dirty linen. One of them, standing in the middle of the square, rotates slowly on herself arms extended on either side of her body saying, The summer day is brilliant but more brilliant still is the fate of the young girl. Iron plunged into ice is cold but colder still is the lot of the young girl who has given herself in marriage. The young girl in the house of her mother is like seed in fertile ground. The woman under the roof of her husband is like a chained dog. The slave, rarely, tastes the delights of love, the woman never.

RAYMONDA ATALA ENRICA
CALAMITA AMANDA COSIMA
GARANCE REGINA NU-TIAO
GELSOMINA SHOGUN ALICE
OLUMEAI GYPTIS NU-TIAO
BENJAMINA SELENE CURACA

They resuscitate those males who founded their celebrity on the women's downfall, exulting in their slavery whether in their writings in their laws in their actions. For these there are got ready the racks the screw-plates the machines for twisting and grinding. The women stop their ears with wax so as not to hear their discordant cries. When they have soaked them in baths of water mixed with acid, when they have drawn twisted beaten them, they treat their skins according to the usual technique of tanning or else they have them dried in the sun without especial care or else they exhibit them with labels that record the name of their former proprietors or that recall their most striking catch-phrases. It forms a subject of unending humour among them. They continually cast doubt on the attribution of a particular phrase or name to a particular skin that they judge too old for that phrase from the chronological standpoint or on the contrary too recent.

The women say with an oath, it was by a trick that he expelled you from the earthly paradise, cringing he insinuated himself next to you, he robbed you of that passion for knowledge of which it is written that it has the wings of the eagle, the eyes of the owl, the feet of the dragon. He has enslaved you by trickery, you who were great strong valiant. He has stolen your wisdom from you, he has closed your memory to what you were, he has made of you that which is not which does not speak which does not possess which does not write, he has made of you a vile and fallen creature, he has gagged abused betrayed you. By means of stratagems he has stultified your understanding, he has woven around you a long list of defects that he declares essential to your wellbeing, to your nature. He has invented your history. But the time approaches when you shall crush the serpent under your heel, the time approaches when you can cry, erect, filled with ardour and courage, Paradise exists in the shadow of the sword.

From pedal canoes in ambush behind the rocks the women attack the bearded strangers when they attempt a landing. They make their machines move backwards if the men abandon their intention, and hide as best they can. Relieving each other as often as is necessary not to reduce their speed of propulsion they operate their boats by means of cranks. One of these is situated at the front of the canoe, controlling backward motion, the other at the rear controls advance. A violent eddy of disturbed water from beneath the canoe comes inboard. The splashes leave white marks of salt on the bare copper-coloured breasts. They stay hidden so long as the strangers keep away from the coasts. They advance openly if the men show signs of approaching and greet them with clouds of arrows.

They exchange pleasantries about what is usually called the choice of husband. One of them cites Gyptis who for this procedure presented a cup to the solitary Euxène. Another mentions Draupadi who took five husbands. Of the first it is stated that Draupadi compared him to the apple of her eye, of the second it is stated that she compared him to the light of her life, of the third it is stated that she compared him to the treasures of her house, of the fourth it is stated that she compared him to a young acacia, of the fifth it is stated that she delighted to call him the rampart of her strength. Someone recalls the Sarmatians, the drawers of the bow, the horsewomen, the throwers of javelins, who did not take a husband until they had killed at least three enemies. Another names those who greeted their wedding-day on horseback, equipped with shields with javelins and swords. One of them stands in honour of the women of Lemnos who all massacred their husbands and made themselves mistresses of the island. Then someone begins to sing, Towards you, my dear ones, my feelings will never change.

The women say, unhappy one, men have expelled you from the world of symbols and yet they have given you names, they have called you slave, you unhappy slave. Masters, they have exercised their rights as masters. They write, of their authority to accord names, that it goes back so far that the origin of language itself may be considered an act of authority emanating from those who

DEMETER CASSIA POPPAEA
TAI-SI FATIMA OPAL
LEONORA EMMANUELA
BO-JI SHIRIN AGATHA
KEM-PHET MELISANDE
IRENE LEOKADIA LAURA

dominate. Thus they say that they have said, this is such or such a thing, they have attached a particular word to an object or a fact and thereby consider themselves to have appropriated it. The women say, so doing the men have bawled shouted with all their might to reduce you to silence. The women say, the language you speak poisons your glottis tongue palate lips. They say, the language you speak is made up of words that are killing you. They say, the language you speak is made up of signs that rightly speaking designate what men have appropriated. Whatever they have not laid hands on, whatever they have not pounced on like many-eyed birds of prey, does not appear in the language you speak. This is apparent precisely in the intervals that your masters have not been able to fill with their words of proprietors and possessors, this can be found in the gaps, in all that which is not a continuation of their discourse, in the zero, the O, the perfect circle that you invent to imprison them and to overthrow them.


One of them relates the story of Vlasta. She tells how under Vlasta's guidance the first female State was created. The young women of Bohemia joined Vlasta and her troops in Moldavia in their scores of thousands. The Carpathian fortresses appear on the mountain-tops with their walls of pink sandstone. In their courtyards after weapon drill the assembled women compose songs and invent games. Another of them recalls that in the female

State men were tolerated only for servile tasks and that they were forbidden under pain of death to bear arms or mount on horseback. At the Bohemian ambassadors arriving in great anger to enjoin them to surrender they cock a snook and make a long nose and send them back, emasculated. Later they put many troops to flight and enter into a long war during which Vlasta's warriors teach all the peasant women who join them how to handle arms.

The women say, whether men live or die, they no longer have power. They are seated in a circle. Some have undone their tunics because of the heat. Their breasts touch their knees. Their hair is twisted into innumerable strands. They say that they have instructed fast runners, bearers of news. Awaiting their arrival they sing, sitting in groups or squatting on their heels, anacyclic songs such as, If the slaves/unwillingly exhaust themselves, standing to insult/their hateful masters/they die but without/letting fall their weapons/too eager for the struggle/to fly and hide.

They say, Vile, vile creature for whom possession is equated with happiness, a sacred cow on the same footing as riches, power, leisure. Has he not indeed written, power and the possession of women, leisure and the enjoyment of women? He writes that you are currency, an item of exchange. He writes, barter, barter, possession and acquisition of women and merchandise. Better for you to see your guts in the sun and utter the death-rattle than to live a life that anyone can appropriate. What belongs to you on this earth? Only death. No power on earth can take that away from you. And—consider explain tell yourself—if happiness consists in the possession of something, then hold fast to this sovereign happiness —to die.

They say that they sing with such utter fury that the movement that carries them forward is irresistible. They say that oppression engenders hate. They are heard on all sides crying hate hate.

The women menace they attack they hiss the men they revile them jeer at them spit in their faces scoff at them provoke them flout them apostrophize them mishandle them are abrupt with them they speak coarsely to them execrate them call down curses on them. They are possessed by such utter fury that they boil with anger

VOLUMNIA YAO SHAGHAB
OPPIENNE LUCY AUDE
HEDWIG LEONIE AGNES
TAMARA FRANCE AHON
SORANA RUZENA SALLY
SU-YEN KIUNG TERESA

tremble choke grind their teeth foam blaze rage and fume leap vomit run riot. Then they call them to account admonish them put a knife to their throats intimidate them show them their fists they thrash them do violence to them acquaint them with all their grievances in the greatest disorder they sow the seed of discord here and there provoke dissension among them divide them ferment disturbances riots civil wars they treat them as hostile. Their violence is unleashed they are in a paroxysm of rage, in their devastating enthusiasm they appear wild-eyed hair bristling clenching their fists roaring rushing shrieking slaughtering in fury one might say of them that they are females who look like women when they are dead.

Great blades with cutting edges like those of razors are arranged in quincunxes parallel to the ground at different levels around the camp. To anyone who arrives opposite them they appear like a series of broken lines. At night they are invisible. Sentries keep watch behind the scythes so that no attack may interfere with their arrangements. The others sleep despite the shots despite the victims' cries of pain and surprise which are heard time and again at different points. In the morning working parties relieve the sentries and collect the portions of bodies divided by the blades in large baskets. These may be heads chests legs singly or attached to the pelvis an arm, according to the level at which the attackers have run into the blades. The collected bodies are buried in a large ditch which they fill and cover with a pile of earth. Then they plant their flags there in great number, some sow flowers there. Standing they chant a song of mourning for the men who have died in combat.

It is said of the army of Sporphyra that it advances like Koo, superb, ferocious, astride a tiger, beautiful in countenance. They say of the army of Wu that it is always on a war footing like Sseu-Kuan of the eleven heads, the many-armed, who bears an eye on each of her palms. The women of Perségame go in groups, sowing disorder and confusion, unleashing around them the desire for orgasm like cat-headed Obel. They say that some of the women infiltrate into the enemy troops, bodies painted blue and yellow, sowers of defeat like the cruel Seumes. From Apone the horsewomen have learned how to stay fast in the saddle and to look after their encampments. The women of Gathma declare themselves fitted to destroy the enemy like Segma the lion-headed, the well-named, the powerful, the drinker of blood.

They say they have the strength of the lion the hate of the tiger the cunning of the fox the patience of the cat the perseverance of the horse the tenacity of the jackal.

119

They say, I shall be the universal vengeance. They say, I shall be the Attila of these ferocious despots, cause of our tears and our sufferings. They say, and when by good fortune all women wish to rally to me, each alike shall be Nero and set fire to Rome. They say, War, rally! They say, War, forward! They say that once they have arms in their hands they will not yield them. They say that they will shake the world like thunder and lightning.


They have modelled their most formidable weapon on the metallic mirror that the goddesses of the sun hold up to the light when they advance on the forecourt of the temples. They have copied its shape and its power of reflecting light. Each of them holds a mirror in her hand. They hide behind the tall reeds, the tough plants of the swamps. They use the sun's rays to communicate among themselves. When it is used as a weapon the mirror projects death-dealing rays. The women station themselves by the sides of the roads that traverse the undergrowth, weapons at the ready, killing all those who pass, whether these be animals or humans. They do not die immediately. Then the women reach their prey at a bound and, giving the signal, joined at once by the others, they begin to dance while uttering cries, swaying to and fro, while their victim writhes on the ground, shaken by spasms and groaning.

THEOPHANO CEZA OLGA
VIRGILIA PORTIA XU-HU
ABAN CLEMENTINE ABRA
HODE MARTHA JACINTHA
MAGGIE URIA DOROTHY
AGRIPPINA DIRCE NELL

To those who ask the meaning of the initials T C O B they answer, you cannot know the meaning. T C O B, they say you may seek it since you have the first letter of each word. They say, it can mean nothing to you, even written out in full. T C O B. They say, if I translate for you, The Conjuration of Balkis, what can you infer from that? They say that the uprisings have increased in extent and number. They say that in view of their spread the abbreviation can no longer be used in the singular. They say that the conjurations of Balkis can no longer be counted. They say that when the conspirators meet they make the sign of the circle by joining their index fingers and thumbs together in that shape. If the conspirators turn their palms outward to make the sign of the circle, thumbs joined below, indices above, it is because the news is good, the war is going well. If on the contrary they show the backs of their hands, indices below, thumbs uppermost, it is because they have somewhere suffered a reverse.

The women cry out and run towards the young men arms laden with flowers which they offer them saying, Let all this have a meaning. Some of the women pulling quantities of heads off the flowers arranged in armfuls, throw them in their faces. The men shake their hair and laugh, moving away from the women and coming nearer again. Some run away and let themselves fall down limply, eyes closed, hands outstretched. Others are completely hidden by the heaps of flowers the women have thrown over them. There are roses tulips peonies lupins poppies snapdragons asters cornflowers irises euphorbias buttercups campanulas. Everywhere on the sands there are petals and fragments of corollas that make white red dark-blue pale-blue ultramarine yellow and violet splashes. Some of the men say they are drunk. They are seen rolling about in the immense bouquets scattered sheaves broken wreaths. They seize the flowers in handfuls and pressing them against their eyelids against their open mouths, they begin to utter soft hoarse sounds.

One of the women relates an old story. For example how Thomar Li the young girl with the high breasts was surprised with the handsome Hedon. They speak of the punishment meted out to them. They say that they picture them fastened to one another, limbs bound together, wrist to wrist, ankle tied to ankle. They say that they picture them when they are thrown in the river, without uttering a cry of supplication. They say, victory victory. They say how pleasing to them is their contact, how their limbs relax and soften, how their muscles—touched by pleasure—become supple and light, how in this wretched state, when they are marked for death, their bodies— unbound and full of calm—begin to float, how the warm water, pleasing to the touch, carries them to a beach of fine sand, where they fall asleep from fatigue.

The young men have joined the women to bury the dead. Immense communal graves have previously been dug. The corpses are arranged one beside the other, bearing a circle drawn in black on their foreheads. Their stiffened arms are bound against their bodies, their feet are tied. All the bodies have been mummified and treated with care for long preservation. The graves are not covered in with earth. Slabs are intended to seal them according to an arrangement that permits of their removal at any time. The women stand beside the graves, the men who have joined them by their sides, wearing like them the costume of peace which consists of black trousers flared at the ankles and a white tunic that hugs the chest. At a given moment the women interrupt their discourse and turning towards the young men take them by the hand. Then they stay like this in silence, holding each other by the hand, looking straight ahead at the open graves.

They say that the event is memorable even though long in preparation and mentioned in diverse fashion by historians writers versifiers. They say that war is an affair for women. They say, is this not gratifying? They say that they have spat at the men's heels, that they have cut the legs off their boots. They say, moreover, that although laughter is the prerogative of man, they want to learn how to laugh. They say yes, henceforward they are ready. They say that the breasts the curved eyelashes the flat or broadened hips, they say that the bulging or

OMPHALE CORINNA ELFREDA
LU-HU MEI-FEI VICVAVARA
QI-JI VIJAYA BHATIKARIKA
LUDGARDE GERTRUDE DIANA
ROGNEDE MALAN CLEOPATRA
AMERIZ BATHSHEBA CLAUDIA

hollow bellies, they say that the vulvas are henceforth in movement. They say that they are inventing a new dynamic. They say they are throwing off their sheets. They say they are getting down from their beds. They say they are leaving the museums the show-cases the pedestals where they have been installed. They say they are quite astonished that they can move.

The women descend from the hill carrying torches. Their troops advance, marching day and night. They say, where shall we carry the flame, what land set ablaze, what murder perpetrate? They say, no, I shall not lie down, I shall not rest my tired body before this earth to which I was so often compared, turned upside down from top to bottom, shall be incapable of bearing fruit. They light the pine-trees cedars cork-oaks olives. The fire spreads with great rapidity. At first it is like a distant murmur. Then it is a roar that swells and finally drowns their voices. Then they fly, faster than the wind, carrying fire and destruction everywhere. Their cries and their fury compete with the noise of the fire.

They say, you are speedy like Gurada the messenger, with the wings and feet of a swallow, who stole ambrosia and fire from heaven. They say, like Esée you can steal power over life and death, like her become universal. They say, you advance with the sun's disc on your head, like Othar of the golden countenance who represents love and death. They say, in your anger you exhort Out, who upholds the sky and whose fingers touch the earth, to shatter the celestial vault. They say, conquered like Itaura, you readjust the two halves of your body, heaven and earth, you stand erect and go shrieking, creating monsters at every step. They say, you leap on the corpses, eyes bloodshot, tongue lolling, teeth fanged, palms red, shoulders streaming with blood, carrying necklaces of skulls, corpses at your ears, garlands of serpents round your arms, you leap on the corpses.

The women address the young men in these terms, now you understand that we have been fighting as much for you as for ourselves. In this war, which was also yours, you have taken part. Today, together, let us repeat as our slogan that all trace of violence must disappear from this earth, then the sun will be honey-coloured and music good to hear. The young men applaud and shout with all their might. They have brought their arms. The women bury them at the same time as their own saying, let there be erased from human memory the longest most murderous war it has ever known, the last possible war in history. They wish the survivors, both male and female, love strength youth, so that they may form a lasting alliance that no future dispute can compromise. One of the women begins to sing, Like unto ourselves/men who open their mouths to speak/a thousand thanks to those who have understood our language/and not having found it excessive/have joined with us to transform the world.


It is evident that the women can go on no longer. They march by continually holding on to their bending legs. Now some fall down. They are seen to weep. Their hair is seen falling the length of their bodies. They tear it out in handfuls and throw it down alongside themselves in masses. Marie-Laure Hibon weeps saying, where is my long hair, my fair curly hair? They march casting their hair beside them without, so it seems, the strength to trample it underfoot. Old women stumble along after them, hopping and uttering little cries, look, they say, all that hair. Then they run here and there heaping up the balls of hair to make enormous masses, some sit on top and laugh saying all this hair. Others cannot manage to climb the hillock made of the hair they have collected. The woman march holding on to their ever-bending legs, weeping it seems out of great fear and misery. Some fall down, no one sees them get up again. Sometimes an ululation is heard followed by other lesser sounds in

HIPPOLYTA PETRONILLA
APAKU EVE SUBHADRA
LOLA VALERY AMELIA
ANIKO CHEN-TE MASHA
SEMIRAMIS THESSA OUR
EURYDICE SE CATHERINE

concert. The ululations grow, suddenly it is as if two hundred ships in distress were calling for help in the night.

They say, hell, let the earth become a vast hell. So they speak crying and shouting. They say, let my words be like the tempest the thunder the lightning that the mighty release from their height. They say, let me be seen everywhere arms in hand. They say anger hate revolt. They say, hell, let the earth become a vast hell destroying killing and setting fire to the buildings of men, to theatres national assemblies to museums libraries prisons psychiatric hospitals factories old and new from which they free the slaves. They say, let the memory of Attila and his warrior hordes perish from history because of his meekness. They say that they are more barbarous than the most barbarous. Their armies grow hourly. Delegations go before them when they approach the towns. Together they sow disorder in the great cities, taking prisoners, putting to the sword all those who do not acknowledge their might.

They quote long verses, We are truly the dregs of this world. Wheat, millet, spelt and every cereal, it is for others we sow them, as for us, wretched ones/with a little sorghum we make ourselves bread./The cocks fowls geese pullets/it is the others who eat them, as for us, a few nuts/we eat roots like the pigs./Wretched we are and wretched we shall be/we are truly the dregs of this world. They cite as a subscription to this quotation the phrase of Flora Tristan, Women and the people march hand in hand.

They say, take your time, consider this new species that seeks a new language. A great wind is sweeping the earth. The sun is about to rise. The birds no longer sing. The lilac and violet colours brighten in the sky. They say, where will you begin? They say, the prisons are open and serve as doss-houses. They say that they have broken with the tradition of inside and outside, that the factories have each knocked down one of their walls, that offices have been installed in the open air, on the esplanades, in the rice-fields. They say, it would be a grave mistake to imagine that I would go, me, a woman, to speak violently against men when they have ceased to be my enemies.

Whether they are marching or standing still, their hands are always stretched far out from their bodies. Most often they hold them at each side at shoulder height, which makes them resemble some hieratic figure. The fingers of their hands are spread out and in incessant movement. Spinning-glands are at work on each of their limbs. From their many orifices there emerge thick barely visible filaments that meet and fuse together. Under the repeated play of movement in the fingers a membrane grows between them that seems to join them, then prolong them, until eventually it extends beyond the hand and descends along the arm, it grows, it lengthens, it gives the women a sort of wing on either side of their body. When they resemble giant bats, with transparent wings, one of them comes up and, taking a kind of scissors from her belt, hastily divides the two great flaps of silk. The fingers immediately recommence their movement.

The women have their backs to the city they defend and face the oncoming male attackers. Their invulnerable bodies, protected by the fire-proof material that clothes them, that no bullet can breach, stand rigid and immobile. From a distance they might be taken for great standing scarecrows whose empty sleeves are not stirred by the wind. The attackers approach, surprised by their immobility. The foremost are mown down by bullets while the women begin to utter fearful cries. The second

ATHENAÏS OREA CHARLOTTE
BRUNEHAUT RACHEL ELMIRA
RANAVALO ON-TA CALLIOPE
THEOCTISTA PORPHYRA GOPA
SCHEHERAZADE ZUO-WEN-JUN
ENGUERRANDE BULLE MEDEA

wave of attackers retreats in confusion. Then the women launch themselves in pursuit and try to catch up with them.

They say, we must disregard all the stories relating to those of them who have been betrayed beaten seized seduced carried off violated and exchanged as vile and precious merchandise. They say, we must disregard the statements we have been compelled to deliver contrary to our opinion and in conformity with the codes and conventions of the cultures that have domesticated us. They say that all the books must be burned and only those preserved that can present them to advantage in a future age. They say that there is no reality before it has been given shape by words rules regulations. They say that in what concerns them everything has to be re-made starting from basic principles. They say that in the first place the vocabulary of every language is to be examined, modified, turned upside down, that every word must be screened.

On the squares where the trestle tables are set up they sing and dance and sing, *Dansons la Carmagnole/vive le son/dansons la Carmagnole/vive le son du canon.* Someone interrupts them to praise those males who have joined them in their struggle. Then, in the sunshine, a handkerchief on her head, she begins to read an unfolded paper, for example, When the world changes and one day women are capable of seizing power and devoting themselves to the exercise of arms and letters in which they will doubtless soon excel, woe betide us. I am certain they will pay us out a hundredfold, that they will make us stay all day by the distaff the shuttle and the spinning-wheel, that they will send us to wash dishes in the kitchen. We shall richly deserve it. At these words all the women shout and laugh and clap each other on the shoulder to show their contentment.

The women say, shame on you. They say, you are domesticated, forcibly fed, like geese in the yard of the farmer who fattens them. They say, you strut about, you have no other care than to enjoy the good things your masters hand out, solicitous for your well-being so long as they stand to gain. They say, there is no more distressing spectacle than that of slaves who take pleasure in their servile state. They say, you are far from possessing the pride of those wild birds who refuse to hatch their eggs when they have been imprisoned. They say, take an example from the wild birds who, even if they mate with the males to relieve their boredom, refuse to reproduce so long as they are not at liberty.

They say, without realizing what they were doing the men have constructed stupas dagbas chortens in many places. They say, the men have multiplied the symbols that refer to a different conception. They say, how to interpret these monuments whose basic design is the circle in all its modalities? The principal building is a hemisphere. Paths encircle it at different levels. One follows them in the direction of the sun. Thus one passes at the four cardinal points before those women of the East who are in process of being born, one passes before those of the South who indicate the light and whose faces reflect it. At the West one passes by those who have triumphed and imposed their will, at the North one passes by those who compile all the legends. After passing by all these an incalculable number of times one arrives by an ascending path at the zenith, at those who record the deeds of those of the East South West North. Their register is an immense musical stave that instruments progressively decipher. This is what has been called the music of the spheres.

They say, if I relax after these great achievements I shall reel drunk with sleep and fatigue. They say, no, one must not stop for a single moment. They say, compare yourself to a slow fire. They say, let your breast be a furnace, let your blood become heated like metal that is about to melt. They say, let your eye be fiery, your breath burning. They say, you will realize your strength, arms in hand. They say, put your legendary resistance to the test in battle. They say, you who are invincible, be invincible. They say, go, spread over the entire surface of the earth. They say, does the weapon exist that can prevail against you?

They go to meet the young men, their groups mingle forming long chains. They take them by the hand and question them. They lead them away on to the hills. With them they climb the steps of the high terraces. They make them sit down by their side on the terraces. The men learn their songs during the hot afternoons. They taste their cultivated fruits for the first time.

The men try to recognize the flowers the women point out to them in the flower-beds shrubberies meadows fields. The women choose names with the men for the things round about them. They make them look at the space which everywhere extends to their feet. It is a limitless prairie covered with flowers, daisies in the spring, marguerites in summer, in autumn white and blue meadow saffron. It is a green-blue ocean the colour of milk with ships passing or else empty. It is a field shorn of every edifice where as far as eye can see the corn grows the rye or the green barley, the orange-coloured rice. The women make them savour the mildness of the climate, identical throughout the seasons, unchanging by day and night.

The rounded shields protect them. Every weapon is shattered against them. Dart-filled bombs and grenades sink softly into their thick substance. If they are at all defective they break at the first impact and fly into splinters like glass. A brightly-coloured cloud similar to a Bengal light then rises concealing the bearer of the shield from sight. It is at once replaced by another, passed from hand to hand. During the day the women hardly change their position. It is at night that great movements take place along the whole length of their defensive front, some bringing up victuals, others weapons. others still supplying fresh news to the entire front.

The young men signal to the women from a distance. They have identical blue garments. Their faces are smooth and round. When they approach some of the women strike up with them the song in their honour.

TAN-JI OENANTHE PELAGIA
LUDOVICA ELISABETH SOUA
CUNEGONDE PAULINE WACO
BRIDGET MOANA MELUSINE
CHANDRABATI CECILE KISI
KAIKEYI MU-GONG MELANIE

There can be distinctly heard the words, Fine martial faces and five-foot lances/on the parade-ground at day-break/to those we name/there is no pleasure in the red costume/theirs must be the costume of war.

Young women dressed in black and wearing masks appear on the scene dancing and singing. They are armed with clubs. They twirl these as they advance. Others follow them with rifles which they pile on the grassy ground. Some are bare-breasted. There is a general movement all around the field of arms. Some carry rocket-launchers. They advance in their thousands. All have a long knife attached to their belt. They sing, The arms piled fanwise on the hills/no less brilliant than the lances of the Punic wars/do not slumber.

A woman sings, shedding tears, My heart softens/when I see the Spring return/Summer grow green again/the sweet air is a mortal poison/the flesh of your lips/is to my mouth/the sun and the snow. At a given moment, interrupting her song, she falls down, she writhes about, she is racked by sobs. At once other cries other sobs are heard. Behind the trees they discover a young man, prostrate, trembling in every limb, cheeks salt with tears, full of grace and beauty. Taking him in their arms, the women bear him to the side of the young weeping woman, applauding when they recognize each other and embrace. Then they express their satisfaction. They inform the young man that he is the first to have joined them in their struggle. They all embrace him. One of the women brings him a rifle, saying that she will teach him to handle it after the celebrations they prepare in his honour.

They run as fast as they can. Some have a rattle in their throats. Others pant from their efforts. Some fall and do not rise again. Then it is necessary to stop and carry them on the shoulders of four of their number. They must run with them until, refreshed, they can once more move on as fast as possible. Shelter is still far off. One of the hardier ones begins to sing a song to restore their courage. She says, Do not hang your head/like one who is conquered. She says, Awake/take courage/the struggle is long/the struggle is arduous/but power is at the end of a rifle. All the women shout their enthusiasm with all their might.

Young men clothed in white overalls clinging to their bodies run in a crowd before the women. They wear red flags at their shoulders and heels. They move rapidly just above the ground, legs together. Motionless the women watch them come. Stopping at a distance and saluting they say, for you the victors I strip myself of my most favoured epithet which used to be like an adornment. Henceforth may you be named in my stead the thrice-great, woman trismegista, you are quick as mercury and highway robbers, skilful at thwarting plots, mistress of life and death, guardian of your allies' welfare. Then the men sing the song of the robbers, The long-haired rebels are united in life and death/they do not attack solitary travellers/they do not attack the weapon-less/but should an official or civil servant come/whether he be just or corrupt/they will leave him only the skin on his bones. The women, approaching the long-haired young men, embrace them with all their might.

The women say, truly is this not magnificent? The vessels are upright, the vessels have acquired legs. The sacred vessels are on the move. They say, will not the slope of the hills rebuff their assault? They say, hence-forward the vessels empty of seed have shrunken loins. They move slowly at first then faster and faster. The women say, this is a sacrilege, a violation of all the rules. They say that they move slowly at first then faster and faster, these vessels buried up to the neck and receptacles

URSULA OBI ATIGONE
ANTIGONE AGNETHE
NO/ SYMBOLS TEARING
ARISE VIOLENCE FROM THE WHITENESS
OF THE UNDYING BEAUTIFUL PRESENT
WITH A GREAT DRUNKEN WING-BEAT
THE BODY RIDDLED TORN
(INTOLERABLE)
WRITTEN BY DEFAULT

ARISE NO/ SYMBOLS MASSED
EVIDENT/ THE DESIGNATED TEXT
(BY MYRIAD CONSTELLATIONS)
FAULTY
LACUNAE LACUNAE
AGAINST TEXTS
AGAINST MEANING
WHICH IS TO WRITE VIOLENCE
OUTSIDE THE TEXT
IN ANOTHER WRITING
THREATENING MENACING
MARGINS SPACES INTERVALS
WITHOUT PAUSE
ACTION OVERTHROW

of the most diverse objects, human spermatozoa coins flowers earth messages. It may be asked, why these excesses? Must they not hold violence in abhorrence? Is not their structure fragile and will they not shatter at the first onslaught if they are not already in pieces from collision with each other? They say, listen, listen, they cry évohé, évohé, leaping like the young horses on the banks of the Eurotas. Stamping the earth, they speed their movements.

Moved by a common impulse, we all stood to seek gropingly the even flow, the exultant unity of the Internationale. An aged grizzled woman soldier sobbed like a child. Alexandra Ollontaï could hardly restrain her tears. The great song filled the hall, burst through doors and windows and rose to the calm sky. The war is over, the war is over, said a young working woman next to me. Her face shone. And when it was finished and we remained there in a kind of embarrassed silence, a woman at the end of the hall cried, Comrades, let us remember the women who died for liberty. And then we intoned the Funeral March, a slow, melancholy and yet triumphant air.